HIDE & SEEK

There's No Truth In Fear

TODD KANE

ISBN 978-1-64184-221-1 (hardcover)

ISBN 978-1-64184-222-8 (paperback)

ISBN 978-1-64184-223-5 (ebook)

Edited by Madison Stewart and Chris O'Byrne

For Jennifer

Just be happy and everything we've gone through will have been worth it.

Thank you *God* – for your *Awesomeness*

Kraig – Wisdom
Cathryn – Friendship
Klay – Patience
Momo – Understanding
Mick – Courage
Juan – Acceptance
Kim — Spirit
Kristy – Support
Valerie – Faith
Unity – Community
Danny – Healing
Andrew – Kindness
Marc – Honesty
Mario – Compassion
Cody – Smile
Z&M – Inspiration

You know who – Lesson

Contents

PART 8

APPENDIX

Words are things. You must be careful, careful about calling people out of their names, using racial pejoratives and sexual pejoratives and all that ignorance. Don't do that. Some day we'll be able to measure the power of words. I think they are things. They get in your wallpaper. They get in your rugs, in your upholstery, and your clothes, and finally in to you.

– Maya Angelou

Mick, Todd

PART 1

She wanted a girl, and kind of got one

My mother was still a girl when she had her first son just eight days prior to her seventeenth birthday and two more before her twentieth. Kevin Anthony, Ken Alan, and Kyle Andrew were the first to bless our family and came at a predictable pace given the effectiveness of the Catholic "rhythm method." This method of family planning used the female ovulation cycle to lower the chances of conception with intercourse. She was on a roll with the KAK acronym and had already decided on the name Kandis Arin for her daughter. It's my understanding that my father was satisfied with the size of the family and argued that three hungry mouths to feed and fast-growing bodies to clothe were enough for his young, struggling family.

My mother was strong in faith and believed the Lord would provide for all her boys and a girl. Despite her attempts to change his mind, my father would not agree to a fourth child. She even promised it would be their last child. It seemed nothing would persuade him until it was suggested that, if it turned out to be a

1

boy, they would name him after my father. This appeared to be a strong concession considering a son would be named without the initials KAK. Her persistence paid off and nine months later, Michael Norman Kane II was born. That appeared to be the end of it as far as my father was concerned. She got her fourth and final child and he got his namesake. However, five years later, I arrived on Thursday, May 2, 1968. My mom claimed she was going through menopause when she got pregnant and therefore I was an unexpected gift.

My mother didn't always get what she wanted, but she got what she needed. She wanted a girl, and she kind of got one in me. I was her special gift, and she made me feel like it. I was protected, favored, and held the coveted title of "her baby." The reality of the situation was that I was another mouth to feed in a family of boys spanning thirteen years from first to fifth.

In all fairness, my father expressed he was finished having children ten years prior to my arrival and held a generational opinion of not being responsible for raising any of us. Life was evolving fast for a man who dropped out of the ninth grade to help save a farm that struggled through the depression and ultimately failed. That life did not inspire my father, and he moved on quickly to begin his own life, leaving struggle and lack behind.

Motivated by necessity and pride at an early age, Mike Kane became a meat cutter at Randall's Grocery in Mitchell, South Dakota. His red hair, bright smile, and energy drew people to him. He was charming, energetic, and determined to provide for his young bride and family. My father was motivated by a scarce beginning and spent a lifetime creating opportunity and abundance.

My earliest memories begin at age five and center around my mother. My older brothers were in grade school, middle school, and high school, and she had difficulty keeping everyone in line. Talk of my father's return home on Friday from wherever work took him began almost minutes after he left on Monday and intensified until the weekend. My mother would say it to me in a positive and rewarding way, but for the others, it was in the form of a threat if they did not mind her. It seemed like we were always waiting on him to come home and when he was gone, I was her "piece of toast" when she was cold, her sidekick when delivering Avon, and her companion when dieting.

The house was always noisy, and it was difficult to go to bed when nobody else was asleep. I'd sleep with her when my father was gone, and he was gone a lot. I was always warm as toast, especially my feet, and my mother and brothers often made me sit with them to warm them up at night and in the winter. I was little for my age, didn't' take up much space, and always had a seat in the middle of it all.

I felt loved and safe-
until one day I didn't

I don't know what my mother wanted to be when she grew up. I never asked. In fact, I don't know much about her childhood. What I do know is that she was the youngest of three girls in a unique family comprised of yours, mine, and ours. My grandfather Al brought his daughter Bonnie to the marriage, grandma Regina brought her daughter Virginia, and together they had my mother, Darlene. She was born at the end of the depression, taught faith by her Catholic grandmother, and when she said her prayers at night, would bless everybody in the world except Hitler and Mussolini. I remember a picture of her as a majorette in her high school band and that she liked to sing. Apart from that, she was my mother, and like most children, everything was about me.

Once a month, I'd line up the little white bags, dropping the tiny lipstick samples inside, filling each order per her instructions. There were always new shades of lipstick to discover, and when I saw something new, I'd get excited and pass it to her. We'd smile,

4

grab the hand mirror, and then she would open it, twisting up the glorious color for our first impression. If we liked what we saw, she would pucker, apply, and then smile, saying, "What do you think?" I'd give my opinion as she looked at me in the mirror over her shoulder. If we both were impressed, she'd wink at me then drop a few into *her* bag.

"What's next?" I'd say, walking each row of bags while carefully inspecting their contents. The catalogs were the last to go into the bags because they were heavy, and we needed products to anchor them down before this last step. We were a team, and just like Avon, we always delivered! I'd stretch up on my tippy-toes to ring the doorbell—ding, dong. "Avon calling!" she'd say with a smile.

We would eat before the rest of the family, often while preparing dinner for them. I'd sit on the counter or stand on a chair while we ate in the kitchen together. I didn't mind the lettuce, carrots, cottage cheese, and diet Shasta. I even drank the vanilla cream flavor. Besides, it was the only pop left in the fridge. My brothers didn't like the taste of it and often teased us. I'm not sure if she ever heard it, but I did. I didn't like it and made it a point to stay by her side and on her side. I was there when she cooked, when she cleaned, and when she cried. She was everything to me, and for the longest time, I felt loved and safe—until one day I didn't.

My father fell in love with another woman and chose to be with her and her four children instead of staying with us. I don't ever remember feeling like we were rich, only that he was. It felt like he became successful and important after he left us with his big blue Lincoln and his big new house outside of town full of his new wife and family. I knew he felt bad about making that tough choice because he came back one night and told us. He had been drinking and explained to my brother Mick and me all the details of why this was happening to our family. We cried on the floor in the hallway with our father next to the closet that housed the big, new Kirby vacuum cleaner.

I remember feeling bad for him and my brother because they were sad. He explained how difficult all this was for him and how sorry he was for it all. Mick and I hugged and cried with him for a long time, and then helped him carry the vacuum cleaner out to the car. I hoped he would feel better when he returned to pick me up on Sunday. I defended him that evening when everyone came home to learn that our vacuum cleaner had also found a new home. There were lots of confusing moments during my parents divorce. I was young and found myself both upset and conflicted most of the time. Things seemed to happen fast, and I remember everyone being either angry or sad.

He was ours to lose

I'd sit on the front porch Sunday mornings waiting for my father to pick me up. I loved running errands with him and watching him interact with other people. I once heard that the person in the room with the most energy always wins. My father always won. There were things to do, people to see, and products to sell. He was dynamic and exciting, and when he dropped me off after our big Sunday adventures, I felt sad like I'd be missing out on something—him.

The main post office in Des Moines was usually our first stop of the day. My father had a box there he could access any time. We would sit in the parking lot and go through each piece of mail. He carried a letter opener in the car, and without fail, would give a play-by-play commentary of each correspondence. I was thoroughly entertained. My father had a way of making even the mail sound exciting. Every now and then he'd say, "What do you think about that, Todderkins?" to keep me engaged.

The car was huge and full of things to open and close, push, pull, and adjust. "Oh, don't play with that son, that's important," was usually what I heard from him because I couldn't sit still. My father didn't seem to get annoyed with me or yell at me like he did my older brothers. Perhaps I was too young to see him as anything other than my bigger-than-life father. I missed him and wanted so much to be near him. Although I was his son, to me, he was the big shiny thing in the sky that brought light to my world.

The next stop was the Jolly Time. It was a little bar on 2nd Avenue, just a few blocks north of the post office. I don't remember ever going in, but he would park in front by the door that was usually propped open. I could hear him stirring up the crowd as he walked in. I was in the car with the windows down. He stayed long enough for a scotch on the rocks, some quick-witted banter, and a phone call or two. Payphones were important in the 70s, and when they were inside a bar, well, that was even better for multi-tasking.

It was hard to imagine my mother in a place like that with him because I didn't know her like that. The payphone was on the wall near the hallway to the restrooms where my mother stepped away to use. He made a call, and when she came back, his voice made her pause and lean in to hear him talking to "her," and all hell broke loose. I'm only recalling what I heard as a child because it wasn't spoken of much again afterward.

The confrontation that followed resulted in him revealing his love for this other woman and his decision to divorce my mother. She grabbed him and pleaded for him to stay. Words were exchanged as he continued to make his way to the door. She grabbed him to keep him from leaving and lost her balance, falling to the floor and struggling to keep a grip on him. Five boys, nineteen years, and too many drinks later, she would allow herself to be dragged across the bar floor as her fingertips curled tightly around his pant leg. This wasn't the first "other woman," nor would she be the last in his life, but at this moment, on that bar floor, he was ours to lose.

I've hung on to relationships and walked away from them as well. None of those choices felt good at the time. Reflecting makes me beg the question, what did I learn from all this? Or better yet, why didn't I learn from it? The answer is that I was a child and incapable of comprehending everything that was happening. I didn't draw from these experiences when making adult decisions. If anything, I withdrew from them when experiencing my own life. I do understand, however, that I have connected with the emotions of these experiences throughout my life and that they have influenced my feelings and therefore, my choices. I may not be able to articulate every sight, sound, or smell, but I can recall exactly how I felt.

A cleverly crafted
bit of one's truth

It was particularly difficult to hear negative things about my parents when I was a child. Comments went beyond what most would consider normal dissatisfaction to downright disrespectful. I relied on these people to love and care for me, and what I would hear described them as neither good nor trustworthy. It wouldn't matter if the comments were partially true or not. As a child, I needed to trust my mother and father to feel safe. I don't believe any child should be subject to conversations that depict their parents in a negative way. We're not talking about Santa Claus or the Tooth Fairy, and the sanctity of my relationship to my parent should have been reinforced, respected, and protected by influential people around me. Nobody was safe from defamation, and I couldn't easily avoid all the hurtful words.

It seemed to me that everyone had something bad to say about everyone else, and it didn't feel good to hear it. A favorite way of expressing pain, fear, anger, jealousy, and disappointment was through humor, a cleverly crafted bit of one's truth disguised in a sarcastic comment or off-handed joke. It was the preferred way to communicate feelings in our home. Someone would ultimately react to the method of delivery, timing, or pure audacity of the attack with an obnoxious laugh, and the situation would quickly get out of hand.

The energy attached to each word would create a crescendo of emotion. Noise and physicality followed, making it impossible to ignore, tough to avoid, and difficult to stop. The altercation inevitably would end in tears. Nobody was safe when this started, and there were few places one could hide if they wanted to avoid it. For me, if it was after dark, I was trapped. I was too young to fight, and the only place I could "flight" was in that little house on East 38th Court.

Ultimately, I developed a sharp tongue and clever wit, too. What was more unfortunate was that I learned how to laugh in pain, with pain, and through pain, storing it's damaging energy like the tension on a bow until an opportunity presented itself. Then, at just the right moment, I'd take aim and release a deeply penetrating word laced with my own fear and anger. It didn't feel good to give or receive in these situations, and when I could, I hid in my room, the basement, or in the backyard to escape the uncomfortable experience. Even plugging my ears did not drown out the sound.

Our family broke apart after the divorce of my parents, and it was obvious we couldn't afford to stay together anymore. Lack, anger, and resentment prevailed, and it felt like someone was always leaving. My older brothers had girlfriends and talked about getting married. They had jobs and plans and places to be. There were twelve years between my oldest brother and myself, and it looked like it was soon going to be just Mick and I left at home. My big brother Mick wasn't big at all but had to grow up fast, and I was terrified he would leave me, too. Everything seemed to be unraveling, and I must have felt desperate to find someone to hold on to. I was everyone's responsibility but no one's priority.

Keep things you care about close to you

Someone had to watch out for me and more often than not, that responsibility fell to Mick. With five years between us, he was just old enough for me to annoy and just young enough to relate to. Plus he was fun, funny, and always had something interesting for us to do. I had a monkey-themed child harness that my mom had bought to keep me from ending up on a milk carton during a vacation to Disneyland. I was the youngest, after all, and I had become accustomed to simply taking the hand of whoever chose to lead me.

That monkey harness fit me for years, and I hated it. Mick had to take me with him wherever he went. To keep track of me, he would reposition the harness backward on me so I couldn't reach the clip that held the lead. Then, he would take the lead, loop it around poles, bumpers, fences, or fire escapes, and fasten it to the monkey on my back. The struggle to get free served to keep me occupied and entertain his friends until I'd surrender and settle into playing in the grass, dirt, or sand. I don't recall feeling any particular way about it. After all, where was I going to go?

I would observe the other kids running, jumping, and having fun. Every so often, they would stop and make a unique sound or deliberate series of movements, like shadowboxing. They would do this for several seconds at a time. One led while the others mimicked and reinforced what appeared to be the most amazing adventure playing out right in the middle of nothing. It didn't matter because I could envision the whole experience with them as they played.

I was captivated by what I saw and was easily drawn into their imaginary world. I could picture bursts of webbing shot from their wrists by the way they were forming their hands. Their enemies would attack, and they would quickly be destroyed with orchestrated moves and special powers, sound effects, kicks, jumps, and even silence as they acted out their individual roles in a magnificent, collective adventure. It must have been even more spectacular through their eyes to be Spiderman and his friends.

I wanted to get up and run with them, leaning forward as I ran into the summer breeze, and at the very top of my speed, shoot a web that would attach to a building or light post, springing me into flight.

Spiderman was cool, but I wanted to be Speed Racer. Speed was a young hero who wanted to be a world champion racecar driver. He would race through dangerous adventures with the help of his friends and family in his father's high-tech racecar, the Mach 5. This high-tech machine had buttons on the steering wheel that activated different devices like buzz saw blades to clear obstacles, catapulting rods that would shoot the car into the air, and wings to glide over all kinds of hazards. The Mach 5 even had a retractable bubble cockpit and turbines for underwater driving! To me, Speed Racer had it all.

I loved that car along with the idea of being young and capable of succeeding in an adult's world. The number five was special to me as well. I was the fifth son born in the fifth month and five years old when I got my first Big Wheel. Speed also had a mischievous monkey friend named Chim Chim. I liked him, too, because he was always in the way, causing trouble and creating interesting drama with each adventure. He never meant any harm; he just wanted to be included.

Like Speed Racer's Mach 5, my Big Wheel allowed me freedom and opportunity to escape when I felt uncomfortable. I began to explore on my own, and the neighborhood became my racetrack. I remember one particular day I was in search of a key to start the "engine" of my Big Wheel and found what I needed in a junk drawer. The key looked like it belonged to a lock, and I wondered for a minute if anyone would get mad that I took it. I decided it didn't matter. After all, you keep things you care about close to you.

One big wheel, two bare feet, endless possibilities

Markey had lots of keys. Keys that he said got him into places others could not get into. Unlike me, he seemed to talk all the time. I was constantly reminded that I should be seen and not heard. All those keys, all that access! I'd never imagined such a gift. I was locked out of nearly everything, including record collections, sports equipment, and even the house from time to time. I was the baby and therefore needed to be kept out of things. I was used to it and was good at storming off with a frown, but once my legs pumped the blue pedals of my Big Wheel, all was forgotten. My whole world opened up over those yellow handlebars - one big wheel, two bare feet and endless possibilities.

He rode his bicycle in front of me slowly and coaxingly, often twisting his body to see if I was still in tow. I followed him simply because he appeared to have somewhere to go. His keys hung from his belt loop, and there must have been a hundred of them. My key was jammed into the ignition hole of the Mach 5 at the right grip of my handlebars also sporting red, white, and blue tassels.

I stopped at the bottom of the driveway as he jumped off his bicycle and ran up the steps to his back door. He stopped and searched diligently through his keys and looked thrilled as he held up just the right one to get into the house. I watched him enter the storm door then disappear through inner wooden one.

I wasn't allowed to go into houses, so I grasped the yellow handles and turned the Big Wheel toward home. But the storm door didn't close. I heard it crash against his foot and looked over my left shoulder to see half a face staring through the gap. "Come on," he said. "We don't have much time."

Bed sheets and other clothing hung on wires with wooden clothespins throughout the basement. The bag of pins was suspended from a string line attached to the wall and an open beam above. It was white with yellow daisies, and it drooped swollen with a seemingly endless supply of them.

The wood tasted like a toothpick, and when you pinched the grip end, you could hear the tension in the spring as it coiled. If squeezed slowly enough, you could hear the wood make little cracking sounds. Maybe not from the normal distance between one's hand and ears, but I could certainly hear it from my mouth. It held sheets, shirts, and socks securely on a line but was particularly effective at holding one's attention when applied to the flesh.

The metal table was cold at first, even though my body eventually warmed the surface. Any attempt to move or avoid his contact resulted in an uncomfortable chill of my skin. It wasn't easy to get on. He watched me struggle with both my nudity and the height of the table. It was impossible to cover myself and scale it. With each attempt, I would be ridiculed and threatened.

There were three grooves in the handles of the pin. My front teeth fit perfectly in them. Each groove had a different degree of tension for me to manage, "Bite. You must keep the pin open, or it will find a place to bite back," he said. The outer of the three grooves gave my jaw leverage, but with an open mouth, it was difficult to manage the pooling saliva in the back of my throat. This also ensured I breathed through my nose. Discovery of this challenge made my nostrils a target as well. Hands were isolated early on. Turning my head was not an option because pins found their way to my lobes and most surfaces of my ears, crushing the cartilage of the left.

It was clearly a hopeless situation to be in, and eventually, my mouth would tire, and the pin would close. "Spit it out!" he'd say, then drag the pin along my skin to the next targeted spot. Resting it there, sometimes pushing it into the skin and gritting his teeth as he threatened me with stories about telling my family. I could feel and hear my heart beating in my head. A pinch, a wince, and then I watched him reach up to grab another pin. To this day, I hate the feeling of cold tears in my ears. In fact, I don't even like to cry. It seemed like that pin bag didn't have a bottom, and there were only so many places left on my body to fasten before he'd get "there." And he'd always get there.

The first time I deliberately chose to connect with the experience was for an acting class in 2008. The assignment was to draw on an experience that would help me cry on demand. I don't cry easily or often, so for me to pull an experience from my past to generate tears made perfect sense. However, the more I thought about the experience, the less meaning it had for me emotionally.

I concentrated on the taste of the wooden clothespins and visualized them connected to all parts of my body, yet I could not feel any pain or sadness. I stood in front of the class as my mind searched for the correct emotion, but every attempt at tears resulted in a rational explanation to myself as to why I didn't cry.

I tried to think of myself as a victim and pictured myself as a scared little boy, yet I didn't feel any particular way about it. Now, I was feeling hot and beginning to sweat. I felt increasingly uncomfortable with the awareness that I was failing in front of everyone. I was supposed to summon sadness at will but instead was overcome with anxiety that quickly escalated into full frustration and anger. I was completely exposed as a failure for not generating the appropriate emotional response. I didn't shed any tears that evening in class, and I stopped attending after that. I decided that tears were not necessary for the kind of actor I wanted to be, and that particular class no longer served me.

When you're afraid, you don't have command of your emotions—they have command of you. I have suppressed the images of this experience from my mind, but my body remembers and has responded predictably to similar situations throughout my life. I must have felt helpless, scared, and responsible for what was happening to me. He abused me, blamed me, threatened me, and then manipulated me into believing it was my fault. The irony of it all is that I had been tortured as a child and did what I could *as a child* to keep it a secret. More secrets and shame would follow as I developed adaptive skills to protect myself, and yet here I was calling on the experience to make me a good actor.

Making milk out of water

My father traveled a lot and was seldom home during the end of the marriage, but there was comfort and security knowing that he would eventually come home. I don't remember everything that happened during that intense time, but I do remember my mother being afraid. She kept me close, and I experienced most of it with her.

My two oldest brothers were leaving the house and getting married. Their girlfriends had already been initiated into the family and had been around so long that they felt like my sisters. Older boys had more freedom and were difficult to control, and with my father gone, my mother left me in their care to keep me safe and for me to keep an eye on them. Each time this would happen, I would get passed down the line, often skipping my middle brother Kyle because he created his own freedom managing to escape as often as possible.

By the time night fell, it was usually just Mick and I fending for ourselves. Dinner was a challenge for us. Nobody prepared anything or thought to ask if we were hungry, so we would have to find something to eat. By the end of each week, there was seldom any protein in the house, and most of the staples were gone or been left out and had gone bad. To this day, I still smell the carton of milk before pouring it into cereal or a recipe.

We didn't buy the instant macaroni and cheese in the box. My father bought in bulk, so ingredients needed to be available to make a meal. Mick would send me down to the basement to find cans of anything while he figured how to make milk out of water. It kind of worked for macaroni and cheese, did okay for instant potatoes, but cereal never tasted right.

I'd eat slowly because I knew I'd have to go to bed after. We were supposed to go together, but Mick seldom stayed in the room with me, and I was terribly afraid of the dark. I didn't get baths before bed when mom was gone, and I didn't like feeling hot and sweaty in my bed, alone at night. I would open the window and try to see my brothers from our bedroom at the opposite end of the house. The streetlight and their voices offered some comfort, but ultimately, I was alone and separated from them. My imagination would run wild until the fear of what was under my bed, in my closet or in the basement just down the street would be greater than whatever my brothers could do to me if I joined them outside.

I'd grab my teddy bear and run down the dark hallway, crawl across the living room floor and peek up through the screen door. There I would always find my brother Mick just outside on the steps. I knew he was there because I had heard him negotiate the spot shortly after putting me to bed. It was a 50/50 chance of getting to sit on the steps with him or going back to bed. More often than not, the older brothers were distracted with their friends, and Mick didn't want to be alone either.

Conveniently devised lessons

My mother was working more and also began to date. This meant I spent less and less time with her. She met a man not long after the divorce, and suddenly she felt safe again. I imagine she felt a lot of other things that had been lacking in her life, and soon he moved in with us. Chuck made a good living as a truck driver, and we all seemed to benefit from it. We had a full refrigerator, new clothes, bicycles, and lots of other things too. We went out to eat at nice restaurants, camped, built train sets and rockets, and I joined the Cub Scouts. Heck, we even bought a motor boat that we could water ski behind!

He would leave on Sunday evenings and usually return on Fridays. We would drive him to the Semi-truck yard where he would receive his freight assignment. He had an assigned truck number and was responsible for keeping it clean and maintained. It was fun to climb up in the cab and pretend to shift through the gears while he stowed his things for the week ahead. Next, we would walk around the outside of the truck and inspect the tires, cables, and lights. It was serious work, and we made sure we didn't miss anything on the checklist. Then, we'd bobtail over to the assigned trailer full of his payload and complete the hook up. Bobtailing was the term used for trucks operating without a trailer. It wasn't a big deal in the yard, but when you had to travel long distances without a payload, you were losing valuable time and money.

My brother and I would ride in the cab with him often sitting on his lap to help steer the big wheel. Hooking up the load was always the exciting part. The truck would shift abruptly in alignment with the trailer upon contact with the tongue plate. This plate rested on the back axles of the truck and had an opening that was wide at first then narrowed as it guided the kingpin of the trailer to the center where a pin locked it into place completing the connection between semi-tractor and trailer. The lighter of the two would yield to the heavier as they coupled. You could both feel and hear the pin lock into the plate.

Brake, electric, and hydraulic cables needed to be connected, the trailer legs retracted and secured, and then another round of inspections. I remember how important it was to make sure the numbers on the cargo seals matched the manifest and that they had not been tampered with. Once a driver signed for the load, he was responsible for its contents until it was safely delivered to its destination. If everything was complete and he was "ready to roll," he would stop at the gate to drop off the paperwork with the dispatcher then be on his way.

All of this was new and exciting to us in the beginning. We were like a team, and it made my mom happy to have help with my brother Mick and me. Although he made a big deal of the details and being accurate, he made a lot of mistakes too.

Once, it had been raining, and he tried to hook up with a trailer that had sank into the mud. He had failed to check the clearance and visually line up the trailer before connection. We spent hours digging out the stands after he had pushed the load several feet back and a foot down into the mud. Other times, he would connect the wrong trailer, and we would have to start the process all over again. Flat tires, low fuel, and errors on his manifest all took additional time, and he would wait until the very last minute to go the yard on Sunday evening. Each time, we would have to stay until he'd get it right despite having school the next day.

Rain, sleet, and snow at all hours of the night doing things that didn't make sense and somehow they would be turned into a valuable lesson that we needed to learn rather than a difficult and often dangerous experience created by his ignorance. It became a habit. Turning his failings into conveniently devised lessons that we needed to learn and opportunities for my mother to support him as the new head of our family.

Patience has never been one of my strengths, and the lack of it played well into every one of his "lessons." We would go out to eat, finish dinner and then have to sit there while they had coffee and smoked cigarettes. They sipped and talked and smoked and, occasionally scolded us for beginning to make noise as we got restless. We were kids, yet everything we did seemed to run well into the night.

He'd tell us to sit still for a while as he watched the clock. If we failed, he would order more coffee and smoke more cigarettes then start the time again. Hands in your lap. Sit up straight. Don't make a sound. "What's so funny?" he'd say as we began to laugh to relieve the stress or simply out of exhaustion and disbelief that this dumbass was sleeping with our mother.

Sometimes, he'd blow smoke in our faces or push the astray nearer to us and leave the cigarette in it. It would burn my eyes and make me cough. If my mother tried to provide relief by moving it closer to her, he would scold her. It often felt like he was taunting my mom to intervene, and by doing so, become a willing participant in his little game. I don't want to give him credit for being that clever but her choosing him over us appeared to be the point of it all.

Sleep deprivation was also part of his game. Physical and mental fatigue increased our chances of failure even more. We would be worn down and placed in impossible situations. To this day, when I can't figure out or understand something, I get physically tired. I feel sleepy and need to disconnect from it. I avoid problems I cannot solve by shutting down.

And it was my name

There was another powerful family dynamic at play during this time, and it was particularly difficult for me to navigate. I was being teased for being happy. The family would add his last name to mine and asked when I was going to start calling him "dad." They would say things like, "Oh, poor little Todd Sloan, he's going to go cry to his *new* daddy." I felt guilty for enjoying all the new things in our life.

To make matters worse, my father's youngest stepdaughter had strawberry blond hair, and my family said she was really *his* daughter. It broke my heart because she was younger, a girl, and had red hair like him. If I failed him, she would easily take my place in his heart.

My name was my birthright, and she couldn't have it unless she really was his. She was living in that big house with him, having dinner at his table, sitting with him in his chair, and hearing the play-by-play at the post office spending what I thought was all the time in the world he wasn't spending with me. That was *my* father and it was *my* name! I was a Kane, after all, and that seemed to be the only thing that would always connect me to him. I believed I was the only one loyal to him and that they were stripping that away from me.

I felt I had to resist and not accept the new family dynamic. My loyalty was being questioned and that was tied to my very identity. I was fragile. I had secrets, and I already felt like I wouldn't be loved if they knew what was happening in a basement just one block over. I had gotten good at pleasing everyone, but in this instance, I could not. I had to choose, and this became a lesson in the futility of standing your ground as a child.

I began to act out and that caused friction. I was being unappreciative, and it brought punishment that was also used by my stepfather to manipulate my mother. My family picked up on what was going on, but it only caused more conflict between them and my mother. My stepfather felt challenged and took out his frustration on my mother, Mick, and me.

Together, side by side

Soon, it all became about power; my stepfather convinced us that he had it and that we did not. Everything intensified with our move from the city to a small town nearly an hour away from my older brothers. It was a trailer park, an "investment" he called it with a lot of potential. The property was gigantic to me as a child and even with all that space, I couldn't help but feel trapped.

The property consisted of our three-bedroom-home, six-car barn-like garage, storm shelter, small shed, and individual lots for thirty-seven mobile homes. My stepfather saw it as an investment opportunity while Mick and I saw it as work. Our summers were spent mowing the five-acre, time-consuming, moral-breaking, summer-ruining prison for at least three days out of every week. When it rained, we would have to stop, and that meant mowing and trimming for additional days just to catch up. We push-mowed it for the first couple years together, side by side with me staggered to Mick's left so that the discharged clippings would not overlap.

It was hard work, but Mick and I did it together like most everything else, and like everything else, we did our best to make it fun. Mick would create the pattern, and on the second pass,

I would fall in behind to follow his lead. There was something about getting the last square of grass after all that work, and I'd look for just the right opportunity to make my move and cross the finish line ahead of my brother. It felt like the Indianapolis 500 where it all and came down to a race for the finish.

We traveled around and around for hours, seldom changing positions, stopping for fuel as needed. It was also a race against the clock because we could not mow in the dark, and to think about consuming one more day on this "track" was motivation to sprint to the finish. My adrenaline would kick in and my little legs find strength as I leaned into the mower, dropping out of formation to make my pass. I knew I had to get as much momentum as possible to sustain the sprint past him before he accelerated, or he would out-run me.

Off I went, eyes fixed on that last bit of grass and the "check-ered flag." I swung out of position and "dropped the hammer" pumping my legs and propelling my lawn mower past my brother, blowing clippings over his already grass-stained shoes and socks, alerting him to the challenge. Sweat dripping from our faces, grass blowing everywhere, mowers bouncing and bumping into each other. We used every last bit of energy we had to finish. Right at the end, we would push our mowers with one last thrust past the line to ensure a clean finish before the hand-safety release killed the motors, and then we'd fall to the grass laughing, cheering, and arguing about who actually won.

He always made it close, and it didn't really matter who won just as long as we were done. Misery loves company, and I loved my brother Mick like Christmas. We took pride in our work, and it was gratifying to complete such an enormous task together. We were Kane's, after all, and despite what had happened to our family, we were proud to have a name our stepfather thought of as a four-letter word.

And so I would fail

Celebrations were short-lived, and we learned not to have them in front of him. He didn't like us to be happy or to feel accomplished, and all it took to remind us was his inspection of our work. A patch of grass here, missed trimmings there, a tool left out or put away improperly. The garage was always a good place to find error and fault. Inevitably, something was wrong, and that demanded a lesson. If we resisted, disagreed, or argued, he would intensify his scrutiny. Ultimately, there was nothing we could do to satisfy him.

We would work for hours moving this over here and that over there. Restack this, wash that, redo, undo—again and again and again. It was never enough, and it was never right. Even when we tried to do it exactly as he asked, it wasn't good enough. Eventually, I lost all confidence in my ability to meet his expectations, freezing up mentally, physically, and emotionally until he would grab my hands and move them to the task as he yelled instructions at me. I promise I would have done it exactly as he wanted if he only knew what he wanted.

And so I would fail. He would make me pull my pants and underwear all the way down to my ankles and stand there with his hand on me. I felt exposed and embarrassed as he proceeded to tell me why I deserved what was about to happen. Often, he'd make me repeat the charges and then explain in more detail what he imagined I had failed to do. I would struggle to get that correct, too. I'd ask him what he wanted me to say, searching for the right words and emotion to avoid the strike. I would even lie if I felt it was what he wanted to hear. I just wanted it to end. It wasn't validation if he had to tell me what to say; I had to know the answer in order to confirm his authority.

There were always specific instructions given as to how I was to receive my punishment. But, of course, I wouldn't follow them properly, standing incorrectly, crying, or trying to cover myself. With each failure on my part, he grew more emboldened and angrier, beginning to involve my brother and eventually our mother in the abuse.

He would watch me struggle with both my nudity and shame. I had failed to do something that was impossible because of changing standards or moods, so therefore I deserved whatever punishment he deemed appropriate. When it was spontaneous, Mick would jump in front of me or over me to absorb the blows from his hand or belt, but in these carefully orchestrated situations, he had complete control.

He would make me lay across his lap, resting his hand on me for a long period of time before striking me. It would sting, and he would wait with his hand on me between slaps and give more testimony to my crime. That was almost worse because it let the sting set in and the anticipation of more strikes build. He'd even ask me if I was ready for the next round. Pause, and then just let loose. I would try to reach back and block or move away, but I was suspended on his knees. He would tighten his grip on my wrists or bend my arms to restrain me, but if that didn't work, he would just start hitting my back. At that point, I didn't care that I was exposed; I just wanted the assault to end.

When it was done, I would run down the hallway to the bathroom, shut the door, and pull the drawer out to block it from opening. I'd gently place a cool, wet washcloth on the hand-shaped welts. They were bright red against my pale Irish skin, and I could feel the heat radiate through the washcloth just seconds after laying it on my body. I would stay in there as long as I could. I was both embarrassed and ashamed to be seen by everyone, yet I didn't want to be left out or alone, so I would go back out and join them in whatever was happening next.

PART 2

Different

It doesn't surprise me that different things are kept in separate places. Look at the supermarket, pet store, your wallet, or closet— wait, maybe not your closet. We separate and combine objects, thoughts, and feelings to establish order and make sense of them. Safety, convenience, and function are all logical categories, yet some things just don't seem to fit anywhere.

I felt different for as long as I can remember, and being in a household where people were critical of mistakes and differences made me feel out of place. I didn't fully understand what happened with the neighbor boy, but I was led to believe that people would reject me because I participated. I didn't have the intellect or emotional maturity to make the distinction between victim and participant. All I knew was that being a faggot or cocksucker was something I didn't want to be. I wanted to be liked and loved, and I certainly didn't want to be one of "those" people.

As children, we express ourselves openly and honestly by exploring, learning, and experiencing everything we can without hesitation until we run into the belief systems and fears of others. When we lead with fear, it's difficult for love, patience, and compassion to prevail. Masking emotions with humor and sarcasm are also signs that we are uncomfortable, and the lack of honesty hidden in the jokes and words causes confusion, anxiety and damage.

We hold beliefs and instinctively defend them as representations of who we are, yet we don't always take the time to articulate them. In fact, with all the information we're bombarded with these days, it's easy just to adopt a belief and its associated emotions without ever forming our own opinion of it.

It is becoming more and more difficult to filter what we see and hear. We think we are tuning out influence, but infiltrating our thoughts has evolved into both an art and a science. We are constantly told what to do, think, and feel on both the conscious and subconscious levels, absorbing external thoughts, beliefs, and ideas without conscious objection or confirmation. If you hear something enough, you begin to believe it and defend it as if it originated with you. You may have been motivated by a comment to spontaneously express an opinion based on what you were feeling at that very moment. It may have felt rewarding to express, but when challenged by someone with a different opinion, you found it difficult to articulate and defend.

Political conversations are a great example of this. Polarization of thought heightens emotions, making it difficult to talk our way around or through an argument. It becomes obvious to the other person and us when we are not certain or prepared to defend our beliefs. One party gets anxious and defensive while the other gets excited and emboldened.

The same is true for religion and sexuality. Both topics are complex and often contradict each other, so it's easy to escalate a conversation into an argument with sarcasm and anger. We have become a win or lose society with no room in the middle for compromise. Losing is so awful that nothing ever really ends. If we lose, we go on and on about how the results were skewed and how we got screwed. It's exhausting and promotes strife and victimization. We've become desensitized to influence and manipulation because they are so skillfully employed to control us, and when we find ourselves at a loss for words or simply at a loss, most of us will choose pride over integrity every time.

Words

In families, fears are easily expressed as corrections by people we love and trust to teach, guide and protect us. These seemingly harmless acts intended to correct behavior can have lasting and devastating effects if they conflict with strong feelings of identity. I knew I had feelings for other boys that were different from those of my brothers. The sexual abuse carried out by the neighbor boy and by my stepfather made me feel shameful, guilty, and confused about relationships, trust, and the act of sex itself.

The conflict was further amplified by the way other important men in my family responded to the issue of homosexuality. Words matter, and children pay attention to how those words make them feel. Let's see if this resonates with you.

A young boy spends the morning with his mother in the kitchen; baking, cleaning and preparing a meal because his father wants him out of the family room while he watches a televised football game with his friends. The boy shows little interest in sports and is easily distracted, so it makes sense for the father to keep him out of the way.

In the kitchen, he connects with his mother and enjoys her undivided attention. They work together and share the experience of making snacks for his father and friends. When the food is ready, he is eager and proud to share what they have created, so with his apron on and spatula in hand, he slips on her heels by the door of the kitchen. He is proud and excited as he shuffles out into the living room seeking the same love and approval he received from his mother. What will he find in the living room?

"What the fuck? Put that shit down, son. Get that off! Michelle, come out here and get this off of him! Son that stuff is for girls! Look here, boy, do you want to be a football star or a cheerleader? Go to your room and get your football then come back and sit with us men. You leave that sissy shit for your mother. Go on! Jesus, Michelle, you're going to turn him into a fag!"

Parents do and say all kinds of things when they are scared. So where do we even begin with this? The little boy is most likely embarrassed and afraid because his father is angry, his mother is in distress, and the guests appear to be uncomfortable. It's difficult to know how to react when you are confused and even more difficult when you are embarrassed.

If the boy is gay, what he just experienced will be a rough start to his life. For the sake of argument, let's assume the father did not intend to do lasting harm to his son. Let's also assume that the experience was meant to be an appropriate behavioral correction to steer the boy in the "right" direction and not a projection of the father's own fears. The fear of having a gay son in what he believes to be a cruel world. Perhaps he felt the need to correct him in front of his friends because they were homophobic. Maybe he felt embarrassed by his son's behavior and thought it would reflect on his own masculinity. Regardless of the reason, the father acted out of fear, and at best, created confusion and distress.

If the boy is not gay, the experience can be a horrible lesson he will most likely share time and again in the classroom, locker room, boardroom, and perhaps in that very living room one day with his own son. If one in ten children identify as non-heterosexual, this father had a ten percent chance of alienating his own son, a ninety percent chance of creating a potential bully and a one hundred percent chance of generating more fear.

I acknowledge that people reject homosexuality and homosexuals. I also invite people to articulate that belief and own it so we can navigate life together with integrity. I question the intention of behavior and language disguised as humor and sarcasm by all people who do harm to others. There is no excuse for the potential psychological emotional and spiritual damage it creates. Perhaps, the scenario above began with a comment or smirk from one the father's friends or was inspired by a beer commercial. We are constantly fed hyper-masculine material through media during sporting events. Add alcohol and competitive energy to the mix and you have a volatile environment.

Let's play with this scenario a bit so we can connect some dots. Most of us have seen a bragging exchange between two men escalate into arguments and bullying. Emotions run high and easily transfer to other guests, spouses, and children in the room. This hyper-masculine environment can be overwhelming and is created to protect the "sanctity" of childlike behavior among males of all ages. It also encourages and fosters dominance among men. Young boys are made extensions of their father's masculinity through athletic, social, and family experiences that often end with a high-five by the father and his prodigy despite being inappropriate and disrespectful to others around them.

There's more to the lesson for all who experience it. Women are often disrespected, minimized, and excluded as this "harmless" display of immaturity is played off with a smile and tolerated without active objection due to fear. This is done, not as a form of acceptance, but in compliance with the behavior as to not challenge a man in certain situations that could make him feel emasculated or embarrassed in the presence of other men. There is also an actual buy in to the behavior called a patriarchal bargain in which minority groups accept and even validate the behavior to receive some type of reward or benefit from a man's status. It's uncomfortable for nearly everyone experiencing it, but somehow it is allowed to continually foster immature and obnoxious behavior by heterosexual men with a myriad of deficiencies. Okay, that's a bit unfair, but this bro is all charged up, and I figured why not vent a bit. Let's just high-five and play it off.

Perhaps the father was uncomfortable with what he saw and felt the same was true for his friends. Fear has a collective property to it. When it is present, emotions intensify, drawing all manner of insecurity to it until there is a heightened state of alert affecting everyone around it. The father chose to react the way he did, and in doing so, neglected the emotional well-being of his son. That encounter created a powerful and detrimental experience for this boy, and the same may be true for his guests confirming or strengthening their own fears. Imagine the new relationship dynamic created between father and son in that moment.

It's difficult for heterosexuals to develop confidence and healthy self-esteem with universal challenges of weight, economic status, pimples, braces, etc. Now, add skin color and sexual orientation to the mix, and you've created an intolerant environment that pushes kids away from potentially the most valuable source of love and support they know—their family.

It's not enough to have the mother be the only safe place for difference in a family. Nor is the family enough to first protect difference and then develop it into uniqueness and authenticity. Institutions can do better to acknowledge and support sexual minorities with inclusive, healthy environments that promote equality. We're becoming more and more about our differences and less and less about the similarities that could unite us. We can shed light on this game of hide and seek if we acknowledge our fears, educate ourselves and support each other in a way that leave nobody in the dark.

We can be very cruel to each other. The shame, persecution, and torment inflicted on LGBTQ+ people and *all* people considered different is unconscionable. You may be thinking this does not happen in your house; however, the problem with fear, ignorance, and hate is that it doesn't always present itself in the home. Unless you deliberately discuss issues of diversity and equality to educate your family, it may very well be a common part of their daily life at school, work, or play. If it is important to you, and you are in a position to influence those you love, then take the time to form an opinion, articulate a belief, and share it to positively influence others.

Back to the boy... now afraid and conscious of his difference, he may now begin to modify his behavior to avoid another situation like that. He's going to want to express himself in ways that feel natural to him, but with each uncomfortable experience, he will chose to hide rather than live his truth. As a result, he may pull away from his family, friends, and even his faith to remain safe.

It does not take long to associate different with bad or wrong when we hear hurtful words targeting a belief or lifestyle. Just because you don't use those words doesn't mean you are accepting, but you can become a threat if you allow them to be spoken. Your lack of action does not go unnoticed, especially when we're looking to make you an ally or threat. This is where fear is emphasized. Not only within our families but our communities too. I remember being afraid and having doubts about those who should love and protect me. Peter loved Christ yet denied him three times. Judas filled his pockets with gold to play his part. What role are you playing in the crucifixion of difference?

Manipulate

Every victim needs a perpetrator; they don't even have to be willing. I'm so sensitive to manipulation that I physically get ill when I witness it. Sometimes, the manipulator doesn't even recognize the behavior until they get the hang of it, and then it becomes a tool to gain the illusion of control. Manipulators love being the victim by creating victories out of your loss in such a way that you're not even sure how it happened. You find yourself feeling sorry or responsible for a reason you can't explain. Other times, you get angry but realize that if you express your feelings, you will appear insensitive or accusatory. Manipulation creates confusion, doubt, and frustration, all of which are part of the manipulator's game.

People who manipulate have an incredible sense of situations and are quick to take advantage of any opportunity for gain. It happens so fast that most people don't even know how to respond. It's very difficult to realize you are being manipulated because even if you consider the possibility, your ego kicks in, convincing you otherwise.

Most of us do not want to admit we were unknowingly influenced. Even the thought of asking others makes us feel foolish.

To realize what is happening, we have to separate ourselves from the situation and think in a manipulating way, which doesn't feel good and makes us doubt ourselves even more. If we are fortunate enough to become aware, we still face the difficult challenge of confronting the manipulator.

First, they will deny it, and then quickly become the victim of your irrational and horrible challenge to their integrity. Careful now, little bits of truth work well here, and they create doubt, test resolve, and inspire compassion. Any slip on your part will be exploited. The longer you argue, the better chance they have to create confusion and doubt, hoping for at least a misunderstanding if not a victory. Manipulators cannot accept defeat. Regardless of the motivation, it is usually the most frightened and insecure among us that are compelled to manipulate others.

Stop

I began to collect my own keys, and my key ring became as big if not bigger than Markey's. Every encounter with him didn't always end in his basement with my body covered in clothespins, but he always found a way to inflict pain upon me. I don't remember how long the abuse lasted, but I know it ended when I was seven because that was the year I began to ride my bicycle. Perhaps I felt bigger than before or more his equal because I was no longer in tow on my BigWheel.

Regardless, something changed the dynamic between us, and I was beginning to test his authority and control over me. I would follow him like before but then break off and speed away for a bit. Sometimes, I'd follow him right to his driveway and then simply ride past his house altogether. I'd see how far I could get before he looked for me at the door and saw I was not behind him.

It felt good to taunt him, but it always came at a price. He would chase and overtake me positioning his bicycle right in front of mine and then slow down, making it difficult for me to stay upright. My feet reached the pedals, but they did not reach the ground, and if couldn't maintain enough speed to keep my balance, I would have to abandon the pedals and get off my seat to keep from falling over.

Once, he stopped abruptly, and I ran into the back of his bike, sliding off the seat on to the center bar. As if that didn't hurt enough, I fell, scraping my knee and the palms of my hands. It would be a while before I would build enough confidence to test him again.

Even though I was afraid, it felt good to be defiant. I was beginning to defy my brothers and mother, too. I was learning the power of secrets and the influence they had over people, including myself. Unfortunately, I was a quick learner and began finding advantages wherever I could.

One day, I waited on the sidewalk just a couple houses down from mine and let him ride by. When he looked back, I stuck out my tongue then took off toward my house. Of course, he followed me. I peddled my bicycle as fast as I could, but he was gaining on me. When I got to the driveway, I jumped off my bike, letting it glide into the yard and fall as I continued to run toward our backyard. I had left my brother Mick sitting there working on his skateboard just minutes before and was hoping he would still be there.

I heard Markey's bike fall to a stop in the driveway, and that meant he was running right behind me now. I just needed to get past the back gate, and despite running as fast as I possibly could at seven years old, the boy was gaining on me. I grabbed the gate as I rounded the corner just in time to escape his grasp, entering the backyard to find my brother right where I had left him. It's all in slow motion now as I stopped halfway between them both.

Markey came around the corner at full speed, grabbing my shirt with both hands and jerking my body in the direction of his momentum with such force that my head and arms lagged briefly behind. My arms reached for my brother, and my face expressed complete terror before the laws of physics demanded they meet violently with the rest of my body on the ground. The impact knocked the wind out of me, and I was stuck between breaths. It feels like your lungs have collapsed, and you're stuck in a forced exhale that causes your diaphragm to spasm, preventing you from inhaling. There is not enough air in your lungs to cry for help, and all you can do is hope to relax or have someone raise your arms above your head. It's a horrible feeling.

I laid there face down and breathless with only the ringing in my ears to focus on, when I saw Markey's body hit the ground just a few feet from mine. My brother's fists seemed to come from everywhere as they struck his face, head, arms, and chest. Markey's mouth was screaming for Mick to stop as he tried to protect himself from the blows. He was looking at me now, both of us lying on the ground with tears in our eyes. I saw the look of fear on his face, but it gave me no comfort. I just wanted it all to stop.

I moaned with whatever I had left in my lungs, and Mick stopped the assault, releasing him to attend to me. He grabbed my hands and pulled me up off the ground, and with my arms over my head, I was able to draw in a long breath. I watched Markey run away, leaving behind only blood and a few keys in the grass. He never touched me again. "Are you okay, little brother?" Mick said. I didn't say anything.

I don't believe manipulation begins with malicious intent. It may even be born out of necessity, evolving as a coping mechanism for the powerless. I also believe it's a learned behavior. We all try to influence others in one way or another, especially children. The question of its morality lay in the intention: manipulate or influence?

Once a manipulator gets the hang of it and realizes everyone has doubts and insecurities to exploit, they'll employ it every chance they get. Lack integrity or feel "less than," and you can easily become prey. Share your failures and fears with someone insecure, and you can easily be victimized. I thought I could keep from being hurt by simply avoiding people altogether. I was wrong.

Game

As a child, I loved the game of hide and seek. It was fun, exciting, and suspenseful. You didn't need equipment, uniforms, or a special field to play on, and you could skip that awkward practice of picking teams. All you needed was at least one friend, the ability to count to ten, and the phrase, "Ollie, Ollie, all in free" and "Come out, come out, wherever you are."

If you really wanted to be good at it, a sense of adventure and some courage helped, too. After all, there were only so many bushes you could hide under or trees you could hide behind. You know what I'm talking about, the one tree with four kids all trying to hide behind it, fooled by the idea of safety in numbers. I'd laugh and run right by. For me, it was sheds, garages, and other places you could really get lost in. It made sense to find the darkest places, too. After all, nobody really wanted to follow you in there.

I once wandered into a garage with lots of opportunities. There was a woodpile, bicycles, a riding lawnmower, and even a canoe. I scurried around trying to find just the right spot to hide, but nothing seemed to obscure me enough to feel safe. I could hear the kids laughing, screaming, and running around. I looked over and saw large pieces of paneling leaning against the wall with just enough space for me to slide behind—and then I thought spiders, cockroaches, rats… hmm, maybe not. But the voices were getting closer, and I was certain I was going to be caught. Despite my fear, I decided it was worth the risk.

I made a run for it. I hit the wall with my back and led with my leg as I slid in behind the panels. I felt a sharp pain on my leg. It burned, and I winced, but before I could connect with it, I heard, "I know you're in here! I see you." I stayed silent and still, even holding my breath. He searched and said again, "I know you're in here." The only other thing I could hear other than his voice was the beating of my heart as I froze and disappeared into my hiding place. I'm sure he searched for only a few seconds before leaving, but for me, it seemed like a lifetime.

When I felt safe enough to focus and come back into my body, the pain in my leg started to burn. I pulled myself out to find a deep gash on the outside of my leg. Blood had filled my sock and had run down into my shoe. I followed the blood trail back behind the paneling to find a large saw leaning against the wall. My sock was red, and my foot was wet with blood as I ran home as fast as I could. When I saw my mom, her eyes got wide at the sight of the blood. She slapped me upside the head and said, "What did you do!"

Parents do and say all kinds of things when they are scared. I immediately launched into "cry speak" as I told the story with as much drama as I could. When I was done, she wiped the tears from my face and took me to the doctor's office. That night, she tucked me and my new stitches into bed, brushed the hair off my forehead, and said, "Honey, you have to be careful playing that game. Hiding in dark places, you never know what you will find in there—forgotten things, broken things, and even dangerous things." Boy, was she right.

The fear of getting tagged in a child's game is different from the fear of being discovered, ridiculed, and rejected at any age. And when we hide as children and adults to avoid pain and shame, we create barriers that may protect us from harm but also block out valuable experiences and isolate us from healthy support.

Isolate

One way we hide is to isolate ourselves by avoiding family functions, team sports, social gatherings, and spiritual activities. We make all manner of excuses to avoid a kid, uncle, cousin, or coach who makes us feel uncomfortable. To us, the choice makes perfect sense, but to others, it appears unreasonable and unacceptable given their lack of knowledge. I'd say, "lack of understanding," but the isolator hides the reason. That's the whole point of detaching, to protect the secret.

This creates an even more complicated situation for everyone involved. Questions like, "Why don't you play sports like your brother?" or "Why don't you find a nice girl like your brother?" For a person hiding their sexual identity, these questions only serve to drive them deeper into hiding. And when our answers fail to convince others that we're okay with our choices despite their objections, we lie, finding the words to appease them and create the space we need to feel safe.

I didn't create friendships or cultivate them. I often stated I was a terrible friend. I'd laugh and say I didn't want to put the work into it. And it was work for me to sleep over and talk about girls and sports and guy things. What if I got too comfortable and let down my guard? What if they figured out I liked boys? What if I was attracted to them? Staying over or hanging out with other guys was dangerous for me. If something went wrong, I would be stuck in an uncomfortable situation. Then there was the risk of not responding correctly when homo, fag, or other words were used to tease each other.

It happened once when three of my friends began talking about sex. Someone started in on another about how sappy they kissed their girlfriend in the hallway at school. Laughter escalated, and grab-ass followed. Before I knew it, I was literally pulled into it. I was new to this school having just entered junior high and was invited to a sleepover. I was a pawn in a new neighbor scenario where the adults could BBQ and drink late into the night and not worry about kids at home alone.

His hand grabbed the back of my neck and pulled me to his lips. He kissed me with his mouth open, exaggerating his movements and sounds as his hands rubbed my body. He pushed his hips into me, and we fell to the couch. He was on top of me, humping me, kissing me, touching me, and I was trapped in the most erotic nightmare of my life.

He moaned and exaggerated his words and movements while the other two laughed hysterically. I have a quick wit and sense of humor, but this caught me off guard, and I responded in a very awkward way. I should have played along with the joke but made the mistake of enjoying the kiss for a split second too long causing him to take pause. I saw the look on his face and imagined the word fag formulating in his mind as he abruptly pulled his kiss away. His eyes and mouth were widening in slow motion. I felt my breath slowly release across my wet lips and then, like a lightning bolt, reality struck and I said in my highest pitch voice while grabbing his shirt, "Kiss me, you big stud, just like you do your mama!" Everyone burst into laughter as they piled on and beat the crap out me. Ugh, boys.

The more I got to know boys my age, the less comfortable I was around them. I know now that I was projecting; I didn't want to give them the chance to dislike me. No friends meant less chance of rejection and loss. Nobody was safe from harmful words, and when I heard someone use them, I would tell myself I was right not to trust them. I never learned to give people the opportunity to impress me because I was always preoccupied with finding disappointment.

The truth is that I didn't want to be a friend because I felt I couldn't be honest or share secrets. It was always one-sided and exhausting, and in the end, we both would be disappointed. A friend was someone you could trust, someone you could rely on and share secrets with. You could stay the night, stay up late, and talk about girls or sports. I wasn't that guy. That was the truth in the beginning, and then I just got used to being by myself.

Achieve

Another way we hide is through our achievements. We seek acceptance through accomplishment and attempt to hide our fear and shame by becoming successful and accommodating. Exceeding the expectations of others makes you feel secure because you are keeping them happy and avoiding conflict. I identify closely with the over-achiever because I was that guy.

I adapted my behavior to associate with and please others. I had become a shape-shifter and at times, an imposter. I wanted so badly to fit in and be accepted that I worked hard to look good, act good, and feel good. I developed an outgoing and charming personality. I worked diligently to be the favorite and create special places in people's hearts for myself. With each new acquaintance, I would instinctively morph into the ideal person for that relationship. I needed to feel special, not different, and celebrated instead of neglected. And if I weren't the best at something, I'd try harder.

Alert

In the military, we used the Defense Readiness Condition (DEFCON) to posture ourselves in preparation for conflict. The DEFCON level is set by the President of the United States. These readiness levels are important because they help set and keep an appropriate level of readiness in case of war. The lowest DEFCON level is five, held in times of peace, and one is the highest level, indicating imminent danger. To get an idea of how DEFCON is used, the Cuban Missile Crisis of 1962 and the Persian Gulf War of 1991 were set at Level 2, while the attacks on September 11, 2001, only reached Level 3.

It is difficult to stay alert for an extended period. Imagine drawing a bow and arrow back as far as you can and holding that tension for more than a few seconds. More than likely, you will become fatigued and either have to release the arrow or lower the bow. If you do that enough times without releasing the arrow, you may question the need to even raise your guard again. This is the challenge of remaining at a reasonable level of alert. It takes discipline and practice to manage your fear, and that energy has to come from somewhere of less importance.

Being different in a world most comfortable with similarity can cause anxiety and keep you in a heightened state of emotion. Just like the bow, being in certain situations or around certain people feels threatening and causes tension. People say and do things that put you on alert, and if you have to remain in those situations for long periods, it becomes exhausting. You can't relax; enjoy other people or any part of the experience because you're expecting something bad to happen. For many, the easiest way to avoid DEFCON 1 is to hide.

I needed to feel safe and loved, so I did everything possible not to be gay. To me, my achievements were like armored plates protecting me from suspicion and guilt. Despite all my efforts to protect myself from others, I never really felt safe. It was like I was always at DEFCON 2. I always had my guard up, losing myself in the process of being someone else. I don't think people realize the amount of energy it takes to create and maintain one's self as an imposter.

Appear

Our physical form represents our first impression to others, and in some ways, it is our first line of defense against negative perceptions. We can dress for success, exercise to impress, and behave to assimilate, but we cannot ever control what people think or feel about us. I wanted people to see a strong, capable, heterosexual man, and I worked hard to create that persona. What people thought of me was so important that I went as far as to make sure I wasn't perceived as gay, weak, or vulnerable by exaggerating my masculinity.

We own gym memberships, count our calories, and go to great lengths to pick clothes that fit and complement our shape. It's also important to get the style right to project our very best selves. Hair, skin, nails, and make-up are all consciously thought out to represent the person we want the world to see.

Some studies suggest that men look in the mirror up to twenty times a day and women nearly twice as often. What if every time you looked in the mirror you saw an imposter—a face that doesn't express your true emotions, a body that doesn't attract your true desires, and a voice that doesn't speak your truth?

Feeling attractive is hard enough with so many "perfect" examples to emulate. Those lies affect us all as they feed our psyche with unrealistic expectations. We pick ourselves apart and focus on what we are not rather than what we are—beautiful and enough. Think of how critical you are of your own body and then imagine what a transgender person feels before gender-affirming surgery. Talk about an imposter. Heck, even if you're a straight, white guy serving as the captain of the championship high school football team, you can still not be man enough. Just listen to his father remind him from the bleachers.

The cruelty, with which we reinforce these standards, knowing all we know about the human body and its condition, is alarming. The shame, persecution, and torment inflicted on LGBTQ+ people and all people considered different is grossly unacceptable.

Not in my house, you say? Well, just like the chickenpox, discrimination and other harmful infections find their way home. The problem with ignorance and hate is that it doesn't always present symptoms. And, unless you are discussing it at home and identifying that it does not exist, then yes, these harmful thoughts and ideas could be infecting your family. Words matter. Being mindful of positive and negative language is very important. Bad things happen, and they need to be acknowledged and discussed.

I mentioned earlier that fear has a compounding effect in that it draws other bad things to it. We can't let negativity consume our thoughts, and that's why speaking our feelings is important. Our thoughts become our words and then become our actions. Letting bad experiences go unresolved can only result in more sadness and negativity.

We can't be afraid to address fear in our homes. It is healthy and productive to form relationships that allow us to feel secure enough to express ourselves. Discussions in a safe environment like the home will make it easier to find the lessons in what otherwise would be considered failures. Make your home a safe place for open and honest communication, and it will remain a loving source of strength, understanding, and education for everyone who spends time there.

If we don't make a conscious effort to create this safe space, it is quite possible that your struggling loved one will withdraw and detach themselves from the family, often creating an imposter that serves to meet the expectations of others rather than represent who they really are. This compromising of integrity is the first of many choices they will make to feel safe and accepted. Many believe it's a temporary thing until they are old enough to move out on their own, but the reality is that they are developing life-long habits that will be hard to break.

With time, the charade overtakes us, and the incongruences associated with who we are, who we pretend to be and how others perceive us become insurmountable. The battles we fight with ourselves and others require adaptive skills for protection that conflict with our true identity. Ironically, those skills we work so hard to master for our own safety end up causing us harm by compromising our integrity, silencing our voices, and eroding our truth. What we learn from these battles does not help us win the greater war with ourselves, on the contrary it only prolongs the fighting as we cope with our problems rather than solve them.

Appearance plays an important role in our identity and self-esteem. The imposter we create steadily contradicts with our integrity. We search for ways to support it with friends, family, jobs, associations, activities, affiliations, etc. but with every setback and failure, our authentic self craves attention. It screams for it, and if we cannot resolve it, and if we don't feed it, it will devour us.

Camouflage

Being a U.S. Army Captain was an incredibly rewarding experience and probably one of the best decisions I've ever made considering I had never intended to join the service. My stepfather said it would be the only way I could get an education and make something of myself, so instead, I got an athletic scholarship for diving and some grant money and went to the University of Northern Iowa. It may have been my stepfather's words coupled with anxiety, self-worth, and a learning disorder but eventually my grades fell, and I lost the scholarship. When the money ran out, I joined the Army. I had no idea at the time, but the universe was directing my steps and gave me the structure and sense of belonging I had always wanted. It also became the perfect place for me to hide.

I welcomed the structure and discipline for myself and everyone else. There was accountability, responsibility, integrity, and pride. I had never felt so connected and relevant before. I had an identity; I was Captain Kane, and I was good at it. This was the opportunity to serve, belong, and achieve that I had always wanted.

And then there was the camouflage. The beautiful camouflage in the way we walked, talked, ate, slept, drank, and dressed the same. Finally, I was like everyone else. Yes, I was an officer and a father and many other things, but I felt like a soldier first. There were rules and standards and systems to follow. I knew exactly what I needed to do to succeed and achieve. Basic training was nothing compared to what I had already experienced in my life, and if I needed an answer or didn't know what to do next, I found it in a manual. Everything and everyone had a place, and I was happy to be in my place. Ninety percent of everything I had struggled with in the civilian world was eliminated when I raised my hand and repeated my oath of enlistment. I was in heaven, and I thrived until the better part of me ran into that last ten percent.

Don't Ask, Don't Tell, (DADT) was signed into law by President Bill Clinton in 1993. The policy directed that military personnel "Don't ask, don't tell, don't pursue, and don't harass." This policy was put into effect to override the previous ban on homosexuals published by the Department of Defense in 1982 just before the AIDS epidemic broke out. How convenient. Just over a decade later, under the DADT policy, homosexuals could serve but were not allowed to talk about their sexual practices or engage in homosexual activity. It also denied commanding officers from questioning service members about their sexual orientation.

Although Clinton introduced "Don't Ask, Don't Tell" to move us as a nation closer to equality for those LGBTQ+ service members serving in silence and those citizens wanting the opportunity to serve their country, most people on both sides of the argument believed it was either too much or not enough. The policy did provide protection on paper for homosexuals currently serving but created problems for the commanders in the field charged with implementation and enforcement. The policy challenged the integrity of both homosexuals and heterosexuals—one inspired, one threatened. Everybody had something to lose, and many did.

The DADT policy was supposed to be an end to the military's ban on homosexuals as promised by Clinton during his campaign. I saw it as a bold first step to allow homosexuals to serve and show that it didn't matter what your sexual orientation was as long as you did your duty. After all, I was doing mine and had no desire to come out. I was married with children. I was happy, successful, and apparently comfortable with the choices I had made to live a heterosexual life. But for those who fully embraced who they were, DADT was compromising their integrity and exposing them with little more than a promise of protection.

Emboldened by the gay rights movement in the United States, gay and lesbian service members began testing the limits of the policy by spending more time together off duty showing less concern with the stereotypes that defined their sexual orientation. Cases were springing up all around the world, and leaders were responsible for enforcing the regulations listed in the Uniform Code of Military Justice or UCMJ (that oath I was talking about).

Before DADT, you could go into most bars full of just men and not think anything of it, but as the situation escalated, heterosexuals began to get uncomfortable. Their concern was that they would be in these places and possibly be considered gay as well. A few drinks, a bit of insecurity, and a homophobic comment were all it took to cause a problem.

Compensate

Over-compensating is another way to hide for both hetero and homosexuals. Rather than turn inward, we focus outward using humor and aggression to overcompensate for our insecurities. We go as far as to target the behavior in others that we see or fear in ourselves. This draws attention away from us and, in essence, we become hypocritical bullies, sacrificing someone else like a lamb to protect us from harm. I had been a lamb several times in my life, and the idea of adding more pain to someone like me didn't feel good. I was a sheep in wolf's clothing, and that didn't seem fair. Who would be my sacrificial lamb if the situation arose, and how would I live with that?

Monday would bring new stories of service members who were harassed verbally and physically over the weekend for being openly gay or mistaken as gay. Two heterosexual men could walk to a bar together, sit together, drink together, and leave together, but if they happened to appear homosexual, they were accosted or even assaulted. Those cases fell to UCMJ authority, and I, as a commander, had that authority. It was only a matter of time before I would have to choose safety over integrity.

There was a kink in my armor. Suddenly, my achievements, rank, and camouflage no longer made me feel safe. The fear was back and stronger than ever, and I doubted I would have what it took to do the right thing. That ten percent felt like the weight of the world, and it was about to roll over me.

I became incredibly conscious of my behavior and mannerisms, lowering my voice, keeping my wrists straight, and even walking with a greater purpose. I was careful not to engage in certain conversations or get comfortable and make a mistake with my behavior. I instinctively didn't have close friendships or spend personal time with other men. That had always been a pattern in my life because I never wanted anyone so close that I could get comfortable and let my guard down. I rationalized that it was just one more thing about me. A little thing that wasn't even of my doing, that responsibility fell on the neighbor boy. Or did it?

Integrity

After my tank company, I was offered a second command. It was an honor, and I accepted it with enthusiasm and a renewed sense of purpose. There were new challenges and opportunities to focus on, and I quickly settled into the position. The significant duties and responsibilities read:

Commander of Headquarters and Headquarters Company of a forward-deployed M1A1 Armor Battalion in Germany. Responsible for the rapid deployment and sustainment of combat operations for both NATO and non-NATO contingency operations. Responsible for the training, discipline, morale, and welfare of over 340 soldiers. Maintains accountability and operational readiness of 160 vehicles and associated equipment valued in excess of $43 million. Responsible for the care of nearly 500 family members in multiple military and civilian communities throughout the Brigade area of responsibility.

Although I still felt like I was in a messy political and social environment, I was celebrated and validated for my performance, and that gave me a sense of security until the inevitable happened. A DADT case surfaced in our brigade. The soldier under investigation was not from our battalion, but protocol stated that the case be handled without bias by a different unit within the same brigade. My battalion was selected, and as the senior captain, the responsibility fell to me.

We received details of the investigation during a senior staff meeting. The case was described as unique because the soldier under investigation was facing multiple charges. We were only to confirm or deny his sexual orientation. It seemed like a simple thing to do but having such an issue in that close of a proximity to me was uncomfortable, even if I wasn't responsible for deciding his fate. I rationalize that being Peter by denying my association with him was better than being Judas, so I argued that as the senior commander, I had too many things to do and that my time was more valuable, so it should be assigned to a junior captain. The request was denied, and to make matters worse, a videotape had surfaced, allegedly containing proof the soldier was gay.

Others in the room began to laugh as the tape was slid across the conference table resting right in front of me. You could hear a pin drop. I can still feel the physiological response I had as my boss went on to explain that it needed to be watched in its entirety and fully documented with explicit details. My body began to heat up, I could feel myself sweat, and my ears began to ring. I didn't even want to touch it as I heard, "Let's have a movie night!" and "Don't watch it too many times!"

I took the tape back to my office. So many thoughts ran through my mind as I found every excuse to avoid the task. Finally, I was running out of time, and it had to be done. I had to decide if I should pause it and make notes or watch it all the way through and then write my findings. I decided to pause it each time I needed to so that I could honestly say I only watched it once.

It was surreal to be sitting in what I felt was the safest position in the world watching two men having sex: on a television, in my uniform, at night, in my office. I couldn't get my mind around it. I couldn't decide how to feel. Should I be angry, guilty, afraid, or ashamed? I felt like that little boy standing in front of my stepfather, exposed and searching for answers. I couldn't run, hide my eyes, or talk my way out of it. I had to take the beating. I thought I could just watch a little bit of it and write a conclusion, but what if it was reviewed and discovered I disobeyed an order? It was a battle between a seven-year-old boy and a thirty-year-old Army captain. No, this was actually happening, and I had to get it done.

It didn't take long to determine the soldier wanted this video seen. In fact, he orchestrated the entire thing. The other guy's face was always hidden while the soldier in question made sure he was always on screen and in focus. Nothing was left to the imagination. He even stated his name at the beginning and again at the end of the video. I wondered why this guy would go to such extreme lengths to expose himself. Had he always known he was gay? Did his family know? What kind of life did he think he would have when this got out? I struggled to understand it all, and then I resolved that it didn't really matter to me what this guy did with his life. Or did it?

I sat in that office and evaluated my own life. I was happily married with beautiful children whom I loved and adored. I was educated, accomplished and respected. It would appear that I had everything I wanted except my integrity. I ejected the tape, completed my notes, and acknowledged that something about me had changed. Over the next two years, I held tight to the idea of who I was and who others needed me to be, but you can only sustain that amount of tension for so long. Soon, I would come face to face with my truth, and with it, behavior better suited for an adolescent, not a married man with children.

PART 3

A lie

Were you a good boy today? Did you miss me? Did you pick up your toys? What trouble did your brothers get into while I was gone? These questions were usually asked of me as soon as my mother got home after a long day of me not seeing her. She would be preparing dinner, and I was hungry for both her attention and the meal. What was I going to say? What did she really want to hear, anyway? She no more wanted to punish me than I wanted to be punished. I did her a favor by lying to her. By doing so, I relieved her of the hopeless task of disciplining my brothers. She had been gone all day, and if she focused on them, she would have to ignore me. It was a comfortable co-dependence.

Lies can become complicated and complex as they build and conflict with each other. Infidelity, alcohol, drugs, money, sex, guilt, theft, abuse, and shame create many opportunities to lie in a family. I believe everyone in my family lied. We lied about where they were. Lied about what we did. Lied about whom we were with. Lied about what was said—even lied about lying. And then there was just not being authentic. And since I was the youngest and always with someone, I was constantly called upon to secure the alibi.

Lies are difficult to keep track of. You lie to make people like you. Lie to make people trust you. Lie to keep from getting caught. It's exhausting! The energy it takes to keep track of a lie and the specific person, emotion, and event it's connected to drains you until one day you can no longer emotionally accept that you are a liar and surrender to the fact that you *are* a lie.

I went everywhere with my brothers, and my very presence made them work hard to deceive my mother. In the end, I needed to be compensated for my "loyalty." Stay up late, be outside after sunset, candy, or pick the television program. They didn't care as long as mom was neutralized. Inevitably, somebody's story would not add up or contradict another, and then it just became a race for credibility. It was confusing and stressful. Everyone would be yelling and cussing. I'd run to my mother for safety only to be called upon to settle the argument. Here was the issue of loyalty again. I didn't want to hurt anyone, but someone had to take the fall, and that someone was going to be mad at me.

I know it sounds bad, but my mom was in on it as well. She would buy something she wasn't supposed to, say something she shouldn't have, or hide money from my dad. I'd be told not to say anything. She would go through my brother's rooms looking for drugs or evidence to contradict a lie. I'd be told to keep quiet about it because it was all for their own good. I think she felt bad making me her accomplice, but I didn't mind because I was everyone's accomplice. I often wondered what advantage it would be just to tell her where everything was hidden. I knew exactly what shoe the pot was tucked away in, where it came from, and whom it was gotten from because more than likely I was there when they got it.

As a child, I learned that words didn't really have meaning or value, so I didn't bother giving either to mine. I didn't fully understand the concept of integrity, and so it would always take a back seat to my safety.

I believed in the promise

Broken promises suck. I promised to love, honor, and cherish my wife all the days of my life. I've kept two of those promises and hope this book honors the third. We make promises all the time, and when we make them, for the most part, we have every intention of keeping them. But what happens when things change? I knew leaving would be difficult, but yet I made choices that did not support me staying. I was driven to be with a man. I craved it, and I could not deny it, nor could I handle the guilt associated with it, so I compartmentalized my encounters and detached myself from them as if they didn't happen.

It wasn't the first time I failed to acknowledge that something had happened, to bury experiences deep inside and ignore them as if I were void of responsibility. It was a coping mechanism that allowed me to forget hurtful things and not have to deal with them consciously. This made repeating them easier because the experiences were not adding up or having compounding emotional effects. Well, at least not consciously. What does that mean? I can't explain, it just happened, and it did so for nearly two years. As the frequency and intensity increased, so did my ability to suppress it.

Jennifer and I talked about my promiscuity during that time after some years had passed. She mentioned a specific time when she caught me online chatting with a civilian college guy. It took a moment to recall it. I had completely forgotten about it and could not remember that part of our story.

She explained she had done some research and found a way to access passwords and emails. She said it was odd how I would respond to her suspicions but continue to do exactly the same thing. Was I really trying to hide? It all came rushing back to me, and I felt so ashamed. No wonder I blocked it out. She got emotional as she shared her frustration and disbelief that it was actually happening and that I seemed to show no real concern about it. How did I do that right in front of her? What possessed me to think she would not know or discover or even say anything? You can only deny and hide for so long before the desire overtakes you. This isn't the easiest thing to share, but it's the reality of suppressing for so long. I was breaking under the pressure of all the lies, and I was insensitive, irrational, and reckless.

I got an STI from the experience and had to go to the military clinic to get treated. What the fuck was I thinking? I was married with children. The decision to leave the military was made. I could no longer control my environment or myself. I remember going to pick up my medical records during my out processing and sitting in the car sorting through them so I could remove the notes from the file. What had I become? Who had I become? Better yet, who was I becoming? She said after that conversation that I promised her I would stop and that I would put our marriage and family first. I believed it, and I believed in the promise because I wanted more than anything at that time for it to be true. It was my best intention and hopeless dream. I had already tested the military and survived its suspicion. Nothing could stop me now, and nothing did.

I'm not sure why I'm writing this with such angst. I feel my fingers hammering the keypad like nails into wood. I told myself in the early 80s during the intensity of the AIDS epidemic that I was lucky that I could love heterosexually and would be able avoid all that fear and danger. I was lucky that a life of fear and shame was not in my cards, and everything would be all right. I would have the life every man wanted, and I would shine and succeed just as it should be. After all, I was the baby. The favorite. My mother said that everyone would see just how amazing I was and would love me just as she did. I was her special gift, and I believed her.

Into the hiding space

The best hiding spaces often require you to bend your body and mind to get in, around, and under things. I found some places to hide where I was certain I would not be found. It was uncomfortable and risky at times, but once I settled into the space, I would blend in like camouflage. I never thought a footlocker would be so difficult to fit into. There seemed to be too many things in my way, but with some effort, I got in.

Positioning myself was tough at first, and I worried I would be found. I could hear footsteps everywhere and voices asking about me. I thought to myself, *Please don't tell*, as I settled into the hiding space, pulling the latch down over my head. I quieted my mind, focused on my breathing. It felt intense as I scanned through the gap. There they were! I admit that I felt fear as they approached, but I had played this game before, and I was playing to win.

"Gunner sabot tank!" I shouted.

"Identified," said my gunner as he locked onto the target.

An "Up!" from the loader signified a round was in the chamber.

"Fire!" I commanded, and with a squeeze of the gunner's trigger, a 120-mm, armor-piercing sabot round was on the way to its target. The shell was completely combustible, containing three spin-stabilizing petals that held the penetrating rod in place as it rotated through the boring of the barrel. Once clear of the gun, they would fall off as the round spun with enough centripetal force to hold its trajectory along the sightline at one kilometer per second. There was just a flash as the round penetrated the target with enough kinetic energy to suck all living matter out the exit hole on the other side.

It's astonishing to me how far we will go to avoid shame, even hiding in harmful situations and relationships to feel safe. We use our imagination to adapt and our skills to cope in all manner of environments we deem hostile. The irony is that we muster all that courage and expend all that energy to avoid our real fears, that are in many cases, far less threatening than our hiding places.

Many of us in the LGBTQ community are separated from loving sources like family and spiritual communities. We have either chosen this or felt forced out for living authentically. We find ways to cope and search for support in friends and lovers, but it's difficult to replace family relationships. Regardless of the challenges, our families have known us the longest and are associated with most of our experiences and memories.

This becomes even more difficult when we become sexually active. Unlike many heterosexuals, we have not developed emotionally or learned from sexual experiences in our teens and young adulthood. Confusion, lack of opportunity, and fear add to our emotional and sexual immaturity, and without a supportive family to talk about these issues, we are left to find answers on our own.

To belong wherever he was

I was nine when I met him. It was a new town, new home, and new challenge for me at school. I remember spending a lot of time in detention with him. He had to stay because of behavior, and I had to stay because I struggled with nearly everything else.

Spelling and math were the most difficult. I remember looking at letters and numbers and feeling hopelessly confused. I didn't know how they fit together or added up. I would look at a flashcard and say the answer time and again only to pick it up seconds later as if I had never seen it before. I felt like someone was playing a trick on me, and I couldn't make it stop. The more I struggled, the worse it got, until I would freeze up. When that happened, I wouldn't even talk. I'd just sit there until I was told what to do next. I was always sent home with notes, additional work, and the occasional threat of being held back.

I was quiet, and he was loud. I was dumb, and he was clever. I was new, and he was friendly. I think of him as my first friend, and in many ways, he was the only one besides my brother Mick that helped me through the next five years.

It was different with him. It was natural, mutual, and welcomed. I knew it was "wrong," but it didn't feel that way with him. Years later, I reflected on how the connection was made, and I'm still not sure, but I know he led, and I was happy to follow. I wasn't afraid and distinctly remembered feeling like I belonged. That word confused me for a long time because it wasn't like the "belong" associated with a family or the baseball team. It was something different, and I wanted nothing else but to belong wherever he was.

As far as I know, we had no resource to teach us about what we were doing or how to do it. I didn't think much of it over the years, but now I realize someone taught us and that we were doing what we had learned to do. I also believe that it wasn't an accident that we found each other. It doesn't feel good to be different, and I imagine we both wanted to belong, and so we found each other. There is a look in our eyes that indicates a want, expresses a need, and signals a desire. I'm convinced that when we see that look in another homosexual, we immediately identify with them. Over time, that look may evolve into a useful way of identifying another LGBTQ+ person, maybe even what we call "gaydar," but I think it begins as a look of someone vulnerable and easily preyed upon.

I went for years believing I did something to seek out my molester. I felt it was my fault for following him into the house. I thought I was reckless, independent, and adventurous as a child, but it could also be said I was unsupervised and deliberately avoided conflict at home. If the latter were true, I was vulnerable to his manipulation and abuse.

Later, I realized both played a part in the trauma because my family was unraveling with my parent's divorce. If everyone was trying to figure out what was happening and make sense of it for themselves, then it made sense that I was doing the same thing. The Big Wheel and the circumstances created the opportunity for him to find me, and he did. What was he seeking? I don't know, but if he were simply doing what he knew how to do, he knew exactly what to look for.

I thought I could choose

Homosexuals seek knowledge and experience as they develop physically and emotionally, just like heterosexuals. The difference is that heterosexuals are taught heteronormative sex education in school and LGBTQ+ youth are typically left to interpret, aside from homophobic comments that confuse, distort, and shame us. At a minimum, everyone gets the parts correct and learns how to put a condom on a banana.

While some schools have implemented integrated sex education, most have legally banned or ignored programs despite their developmental value and potential to decrease sexually transmitted infections. Even with basic knowledge, LGBTQ+ kids still struggle with misinformation and developing the social and emotional maturity needed for healthy sexual experiences and relationships.

The lack of education and trusted people both in and out of the home results in a lag in emotional development typically created by healthy experiences. Moreover, sexual exploration is driven into hiding and conducted in a manner that feels good initially but can cause long-term harm physically, emotionally, and spiritually. These normal explorations are linked to feelings of anxiety, shame, and guilt, creating unhealthy associations that are difficult to overcome, even with time and experience.

On the other hand, heterosexual explorations of sex are encouraged and celebrated among peers, siblings, and some parents, while other sexual minorities are ridiculed and tormented. Helpful and healthy information is available; however, many youth are not getting it. The lack of safe environments to identify as LGBTQ+ means a lack of resources to keep them safe.

This was particularly important to me in high school when AIDS consumed the world with fear, confusion, and hate. Nobody appeared to know the facts, and that terrified me. I remember everyone being afraid of drinking from water fountains, touching door handles, or sitting on toilet seats. Add the ignorance and immaturity of teenagers, and you had nowhere to turn for answers, and you dared not ask for fear of being teased or worse. I knew what I desired, but the fear it created motivated me to choose a heterosexual life. At least, I *thought* I could choose.

I acknowledge that as parents, it's difficult when we're asked to engage in uncomfortable conversations about sex, but we have the ultimate responsibility to maintain safe and healthy relationships with our children. There is no app that can substitute the love and acknowledgment of a parent. Without support and protection from our families, we are vulnerable to all kinds of threats, even from ourselves.

It's troubling to hear that there are parents who suspect their children of being gay but still have not had a conversation with them about it. Haven't we established that homosexuality is not a phase that we grow out of? And haven't we also learned that kids will not "figure it out" on their own? In fact, they will seek answers from whomever and whatever source they can. Do you want to take that chance as a parent or loved one? When communication fails, critical time passes, creating doubt and mistrust between parent and child. Meanwhile, children pass through their teens and into adulthood disconnected and often estranged from family. What is wrong with asking the question, "Are you gay?"

Those three little words are just as important and powerful to us questioning ourselves as, "I love you."

Broken people like to find other broken people. I don't particularly like the term "broken," but it often feels like that when you are isolated and have had emotional and sexual experiences that left you hurt and with lots of questions. Isolation leaves us with very few people in our lives with whom to share our stories and experiences, so when we do, we hope for acknowledgement, acceptance, or validation. If we don't get what we're seeking, we simply find another person to listen or tell our stories to in a different way. No matter how we tell them, many of our stories have a familiar theme, and there is plenty of commiserating to be done once they are shared. When you are hurting, lonely, lacking, or shameful, you are thirsty for connection, and a single drop of water can seem like a drinking fountain. They are not the same.

Now let's add sex to this equation. Say I go to a club (hide) to make myself available for a new experience (seek), and I meet someone I totally connect with (find). Now, I will want to take the experience further and have sex. Success? Nope. A couple weeks go by if I'm determined to make something work, but ultimately, I discover he was not at all what I was looking for.

That's not the end of it. We tell ourselves we went to the club to find a partner with whom we could have amazing sex with when actually we went to the club to find sex hoping to snag a boyfriend out of the experience. Disappointed in yet another failed attempt at finding the love of our lives, we tell all our friends what a jerk he was and other things necessary to get him out of our system. Thank goodness our friends have similar experiences to validate our behavior and together we agree to move on and meet at the exact same club next weekend. With the codependent support and validation of our friends, we modify our original story to add the latest Mr. Wrong, and off to the club we go to find the next Mr. Right... Now.

This behavior isn't surprising given the suppressed sexual desires and delayed social and emotional development of LGBTQ+ youth and young adults. Many heterosexuals use the same rationale when struggling to socialize and successfully partner. It just seems intensified in our community due to the lack of opportunity and experience.

A well-intended search online

The Internet is an incredible tool and an easy way to access information about anything you're looking for. However, it's most effective when you narrow your search. The challenge comes when you're not really sure where to begin, and you just type in "gay," for example. If not immediately, then within a few clicks, you're in the middle of adult content that can distract, discourage, and misinform you.

Search engines do not monitor intentions, only history and patterns. Who could blame a teenager or young adult for becoming intrigued by sexual content? Already curious, and at the age of discovery, pornography soon becomes a defunct teacher. Now, they have another thing to hide. What do I mean?

Well, how many heterosexual teenagers would admit to watching or researching porn? Exactly. Now add "gay porn" to the list of things they are hiding, and the chances of getting valuable, healthy information drops significantly. Pornography sites are notorious for capturing your attention by exposing you to every desire imaginable with no accountability or healthy way to navigate it.

And what about LGBTQ+ people and allies—family, friends, and others committed to equality and education? How far do they get before the content becomes too uncomfortable or even offensive? Most allies are conscious of the acronyms, terms, and issues facing our community but even they have difficulty navigating through the traps set by Internet pornographers.

Some allies have no idea where to begin their search for knowledge. An example would be an uncle or brother who simply wants to learn more about the lifestyle or issues facing their gay nephew or sister. A well-intended search online could have a disastrous effect on an unsuspecting person. That fear is real, and the experience can discourage them from seeking further knowledge to connect with our community. We cannot afford missed opportunities like these, so I've compiled a list of valuable online resources in the back of the book to help you successfully seek LGBTQ+ education and information.

Courage and commitment to equality

Many organizations and institutions continue to struggle with policy, laws, and leadership that lack courage and commitment to equality. The LGBTQ+ community has benefitted from the victories earned by other minorities over the years and the civil rights movement continues to encourage diversity and establish equality for all people. As sexual minorities, we can do more to equip and empower each other. Words matter, and how they are used emphasizes their importance and determines their effectiveness.

Don't Ask, Don't Tell (DADT), instituted in 1993, is another example of the importance of words. DADT upheld the ban on homosexual activity, directing leadership not to seek out homosexual behavior while allowing gays to serve as long as they continued to hide. I believe it was instituted with good intention but lacked integrity and resolve in the language. Although it was directed by the Commander in Chief, it wasn't commanding. Both sides were asked to compromise their integrity, and the directive seemed weak. There was hesitation (fear) in the effort, and it denied gay service members the ability to live their truth. Compromises are necessary to move us forward on divisive issues in a democracy but they can't compromise our integrity to do so.

PART 4

I wasn't Captain
Kane anymore

I told my wife first. It wasn't a complete shock to her because we had been here before not two years earlier. I was getting my master's degree, working a joint military assignment in Florida, and contemplating accepting promotion to the rank of Major. If I did, I was certain of a position with an old mentor I greatly respected who had just been promoted to Brigadier General. The new position was exactly what I needed to excel and have access to greater opportunities, but the thought of taking that position and continuing to hide was more than I could take. The over-achiever in me worked and planned and even celebrated the advancement, but the seven-year-old boy believed he would fail and be discovered for a fraud.

An opportunity to plant the seed to work with my father came on a visit he and his wife made while we were still in Florida. It was a soft sell, but I was certain he would buy it, and he did. I think Jennifer thought it was a good idea, too. She knew I was unhappy and scrambling for something to focus on. She also knew what I did to avoid pain and failure, even if I didn't. It was decided that I would leave the military and work with my father. I had successfully avoided the anxiety of failure by creating an opportunity that disguised the fact that I quit. Problem solved.

I left the military and began working with my father at his company in Iowa. Jennifer, the kids, and I settled in Arizona after I left the Army. It seemed like a dream come true. I would be working with my dad in the building with our name on it, and we would travel all around the world and share amazing adventures and make lots of money. This wasn't just another Sunday afternoon visitation with him, we were adults, past it all, and I hoped it was an opportunity for us to become closer as father and son. That was the idea, anyway, and we set off to conquer the world.

We agreed I would work one week on the road, one week in Iowa, and two weeks from home in Arizona. I thought it was perfect because I needed to learn as quickly as possible to be effective and Jen and the kids could visit me and family living in Iowa every couple of months to decrease the time apart.

It was exciting to work with my dad. I had always dreamed of this and believed it would fill a void created twenty-three years earlier. He was excited, patient, and eager to teach me at first, but we were both leaders and full of pride. Eventually, we became frustrated with each other. He had wanted me to take over many of his responsibilities but hesitated to give me the authority that went along with them. I took a thorough systems approach to every aspect of the business. This took several months and exposed a lot of opportunities for improvement that he was uncomfortable with. I also suggested ways to improve each system, and that didn't sit well with him either. He wanted me on the phones making sales calls. I told him if I never picked up a phone again that I'd increase profits by 20% just by un-fucking his business practices. That went over well.

I wasn't being critical of my father; I was being critical of the business. He didn't like what he was hearing, and I wasn't sugar coating it. All I know was that I was there to get things done, and I wanted to show him I was every bit the go-getter he was. I had bought into the persona of my father and tried to emulate him every chance I got, but the more I got to know him, the more I realized he exaggerated just as much as the next guy. I didn't think less of my father because of this revelation. On the contrary, his authenticity was comforting and grounding. In fact, it made me love and respect him even more.

We struggled in the beginning because I failed to realize the company *was* my father and that he had avoided other aspects of his life and even hid from them behind those walls. To be critical of it was to be critical of him, and I know what it's like when someone finds your hiding place.

The first to go was patience; the second was confidence, and finally, my ability to cope with failure. Soon, the travel schedule went off track, and I was gone more than expected. I was over my head and out of my element and on the verge of being out of control. The military had been a complex environment with rules and consequences that I managed to navigate successfully. This couldn't be as hard, but I had no structure, no manuals and no camouflage. And to make it as complicated as possible, I was working for my father.

I didn't feel accomplished, capable, or safe. I was threatened and had no armor to fall back on. This wasn't the Army, and I wasn't Captain Kane anymore. I was Todd Kane, number five son of Mike Kane, and I wasn't getting the job done. Well, that's not entirely true. I was getting the job done. Sales were up; operations were more efficient—but my relationship with my father was strained. I needed his approval because I had nothing else to fall back on. I didn't know how to disagree and function with others. My life was yes, no, do or don't. I was also feeling the stress of being away from home and it became more and more difficult to be present with my family when tied to my father by phone. I started to avoid all discomforts and found distractions online. It was just like before, only this time I wasn't as concerned about hiding. My desire for men had never gone away, and neither did the challenges that came along with it.

I threw fear out the window and caution soon followed. The failures associated with my father took a back seat to a new and confusing lifestyle. Once again, I had substituted one problem with another, rationalizing that I needed to explore my sexuality to bring balance and integrity to my life. In doing so, I wouldn't be subject to anyone's rules or anxiously wait to be punished anymore. I was determining my fate, facing my fears, and would finally be in control of my life. I didn't fear anyone or anything, now, but there were far greater monsters out there than what I had imagined.

Jennifer didn't fight me, attack me, or make me feel bad about it. In fact, she supported me. This time, however, I didn't say I'd stop. Looking back, I hadn't fully embraced everything about my sexuality, my fears, or even my identity. I was still hiding, but from what now? Everything? I was nervous, out of place, and inexperienced, but I don't remember being afraid, more like determined.

Next came the declaration to my family. I realized I wasn't completely sure what all that entailed. I had always been gay; I just hadn't accepted that as my truth. To further complicate matters, I loved my wife, but my desire to explore this part of me was undeniable.

I finally had my integrity, and I was officially gay. Now what? Was I was supposed to change the way I walked, talked, dressed, or other things about me? If so, what and how did I do that? The truth had set me free but didn't supply an operator's manual. I began to feel uneasy, again realizing I lacked the structure, accountability, and identity of the military. I had no idea how important that lifestyle had become to me, and I had no place to hide. I was out—way out.

The red flag

Walking into a gay bar was awkward. It was a dash from the parked car to the door of the bar, followed by a sigh of relief once safely inside. It looked like every other bar I'd been in. There was a pool table, bar stools, a pinball machine, and men. I remember the face of the bartender, the pictures of naked men on the wall, and the eyes that fell on me. The drinks were very strong and soon so was my resolve. Talking with other men in a bar was never this difficult. It was not conversational or even pleasant. It was a constant barrage of inappropriate comments that left me feeling insulted. I'd never been hit on by another man in a bar before. In fact, I don't even remember being hit on by a woman. I was hoping it would stop after a bit but it didn't stop, ever.

There was one proposition after another, and I was surprised at the determination and courage they all had. I remember thinking how every woman deserved an apology for having to deal with this. One guy, however, was particularly forward, flirty, and seemed into me. I acknowledged that the only difference between him and all the others was that I was attracted to him. I didn't go home alone.

This new life was both exhilarating and exhausting at the same time. I had not anticipated how fast things would move for an adult man with time, means, and desire. I was adapting quickly to fit in and function in my new environment. Oddly enough, I didn't ask my family for guidance or share any of my experiences with them. I continued to isolate myself and lie to cover where I was going and what I was doing despite being "out." I didn't want to seem ill-equipped or unprepared for it all. There were lessons that had to be learned, and I didn't want to share those, either.

My family was still in shock, and they were justified. All of this was surreal to them. It was surreal to me too. I was going to reconstruct my life, run my father's company, earn a bunch of money, and buy a huge house with two wings. Jennifer would live on one side, and I on the other, and our kids raised between us with love and understanding. I really believed it would work because now I had the truth on my side, and I was certain *that's* what had stopped me from being successful and happy all my life.

And then the fever came, along with a strange tingling in my mouth, then shortly thereafter the rash on my forearm. I was tired all the time. The stress of it all was getting to me, but I believed it was worth it. I knew coming out would be difficult and that there would be consequences, but the truth had prevailed. All I needed to do was power through it because giving up meant I'd have to go back to living a lie.

Once out, I kept very little from Jennifer. I had met her at age seventeen, and she knew me better than anyone. Despite my actions and the situation, we loved each other, and she knew I'd withdraw from everyone and would need someone to talk to. She even suggested we open the marriage up, accept it all as the truth, and get a handle on it. She was able to confide in her sister, who was a nurse. It was she who raised the red flag about the rash on my arm. She also told her to stay away from me and talk to me about getting checked for sexually transmitted diseases. We discussed it, and I did.

I got a call around 3:15 and told the doctor's office that I could make it by 4:15. It had been well over a week, and I was scared. I drove as fast as I could, whispering, "No, no, no; please

God, no." I thought of the guy I had slept with. I was nervous the second time I saw him at the bar. I was sober then and thought he was a high-risk guy. Pulling into the parking lot, I sighed as I composed myself and prayed for the best but remembered thinking I was in trouble.

I felt sick to my stomach as I said my name to the lady at the desk. I wondered if the doctor would tell me alone if it was positive. I hoped that the short notice to get me in meant he would simply tell me I was good to go and check me off his list of people to see that day. "Todd," said the lady at the desk as a guy sat down beside me and said, "How are you today?" I just smiled as I got up and walked into the office.

"Please, have a seat; close the door," the doctor said. I was filled with anxiety as he sighed and said, "I wish I had better news."

My head dropped to my hands, and I whispered, "No."

I'm sorry; your results show you're positive for HIV-1.

"No," I said.

"Geez I hate having to do this, I know it is a shock. They took so long because we sent them to Iowa City to have them checked again."

"My actions have affected the lives of so many people," I said. He kept talking, and I thought to myself, *I'm poison, literally poison. What have I done?* I broke into a sweat, as a rush of emotions rolled over me—death, suicide, and disbelief. *Hide*, I thought. *Hide!* Then I just stopped. A familiar, high-pitched ring filled my head. I remember feeling as though it all had just ended as I whispered, "I deserve this."

I drove back to my father's house where Jennifer and the kids were visiting. I took a shower and looked at myself in the mirror. I thought of what the last forty-three days had meant to me. All of the work it had taken to stop the lie. How empowered I felt; how freeing it had been. Suddenly, it all felt selfish, and I was ashamed of myself. None of it mattered, now. I went in and sat on the edge of the bed. Jennifer came in and sat beside me as tears welled up in my eyes. I never actually said it, but she knew.

And then you go too

Over the next few days, I told everyone. I even went back to the bar to tell the guy what I had learned. I began taking my medication right away. It was difficult to adjust to the side effects. I was dizzy in the morning for a couple hours. Other side effects gave me horrible dreams, and I didn't sleep well.

I decided I would stay in Iowa, and Jennifer and the kids would return to Arizona. I needed to work, and she needed her family. My father was patient, but not handling it well. I did what I could to stay focused and make him feel secure, but I could tell he was losing confidence in my ability to run things, and this was all beginning to be too much for him.

I remember the night I told my father I was gay. He was one of the first people I told. We traveled a lot together, and he was always very aware of me, making sure I was learning and paying attention to the lessons he was teaching. We were in North Carolina and had just visited a large client of ours. Things had gone well, and he was feeling more confident and comfortable with me now, mainly because I was distracted and had become less critical of the business. Going with the flow of things made it easier for both of us to enjoy the work.

He sat me down and asked what was going on with me. It was rare that my father ever focused on a single thing, but he stopped everything, looked me directly in the eyes, and asked, "Son, what's wrong?"

I struggled with the truth because he was my father, and I had wanted so long for him to give me love and attention. He asked again, and I replied, "What's the worst thing a son could tell a father?"

He leaned in and asked if I was sick or dying. I was surprised at his answer and even more surprised that I thought being gay was worse. I told him, and he replied, "Son, we all have secrets and desires. You just keep them to yourself and do what you need to do."

I struggled with that answer. I said I was tired of living a lie. I said I couldn't do it anymore and that it was just one more thing about me people were going to have to accept. He looked at me concerned but didn't say anything more. It wasn't what I was looking for, but it wasn't what I had expected either.

As it all unfolded, those words kept playing over and over in my mind. I had not put my secret away. In fact, I had dropped it like a bomb and got infected with HIV. I was estranged from my wife and family, living with him, struggling to get up in the morning, and occasionally stopping wherever I was to keep my balance as a result of my medications. I went from hero to zero, and he couldn't wrap his mind around it. I believe he was scared and possibly felt responsible for it all perhaps thinking he lured me away from the military.

It was a lot for him to take in, and I didn't expect him to celebrate, just acknowledge. He even knew I had been seeing a guy for a while and took the time to ask me if I liked him and if "all of that" made me happy. I recognized that as a big step for my Dad, which made it even more important to get everything right. That's what I did, I got things right. I had a beautiful wife and red headed children. I was a soldier and well educated and everybody loved me, especially my father.

I had been spending more time with Juan. I had met him a few weeks before I was diagnosed. I told him, and he tested negative. I fully expected him to run from me, but he didn't. He was very kind. I've always admired that in a person. We became close, and I felt very fortunate to have met him.

He took me to an AIDS benefit. It was a difficult experience at first, but he held my hand, made me feel human, and I asked him to come home with me. I was staying at my father's house, of course, and he asked, "Is your dad out of town?" He had stayed with me before when my dad was away.

"No, he leaves in the morning early," I said, explaining that we would be quiet. I honestly didn't want to be alone. He reluctantly agreed.

It was early. The door of the room suddenly crashed open, and the light came on. My father was in his coat, bag over his shoulder, ready to go—go wherever he wanted, whenever he wanted, however he wanted—and I sat up just to see his angry face before he turned away from the sight of us. He saw what he needed to see, and then said what he needed to say, "You get him the fuck out of this house, and then you go, too!"

"Dad, it's not like that! I just wanted him here with me, I just wanted..." I said as I jumped out of bed. I heard him mumble something over the wheels of his carry-on bag as he walked out the door to the garage. The wooden screen door slammed as his carry-on bag made the same sound going down the steps. The sun hadn't even cracked the horizon yet as I ran halfway down the hallway before catching my balance. "Dad!" I yelled toward him. I didn't see his face, just the back of his tan, cashmere coat, grayish red hair, and black briefcase disappear beyond the door. He was leaving again, and this time it was my fault.

PART 5

Hiding all over again

It was all very new to me. I mean, I understood the mechanics of being gay, but I had no idea how to navigate the lifestyle. There seemed to be no rules to follow, and what worked with girls proved to be ineffective with guys. Not that I was ever really good at getting the girls, anyway. It seemed all I could do was react to what gay men said and then fumble through awkward and uncomfortable situations.

To make matters worse, I was seldom attracted to the men who approached me. I was operating by a set of rules that didn't apply to gay dating. I didn't ignore people, I wasn't rude, and I accepted conversation for conversation's sake along with the drinks that came with them. I often found myself stuck with someone with whom I was not interested because I didn't want to offend them. I was a nice guy in a gay bar. That's not how it works. You apparently have to be a bitch to get your point across, but that's a whole other book.

I lacked confidence, despite taking particular care of how I looked on the outside I felt like poison on the inside. My new friends couldn't understand why I wouldn't seal the deal and go home with guys. I didn't go home with anyone because I would have to tell him I was HIV+. If it didn't work out, he'd tell every-one, and nobody would even give me the opportunity to get to know or want me sexually. That was a risk I wasn't willing to take. Also, I didn't want my friends to know. I didn't want anyone to know. Hell, I didn't want to know.

There was always the possibility of being rejected. Then there was the possibility of being accepted, then rejected. Finally, you could be accepted, rejected, and then marked with a big, red, plus sign on your forehead. I know this might sound a bit harsh, but this was how I felt. I basically went from one secret to the next, and I wasn't even sure how the first secret was going to play out.

I had my old skills to fall back on. Isolation gave me comfort and space should I fail, and compartmentalizing friends kept everyone at a safe distance. There were the ones you were seen with, the ones you partied with, and those you didn't want anyone to see—no connections and no strings attached. I was hiding all over again, only this time I was out. I felt tortured inside. I wanted so desperately to be loved and to love with this new truth, yet I felt even less lovable than before. I was unforgiving of myself. I had let go of my fear, lived with integrity, played with fire, and gotten burned.

To add to the guilt and shame, I had made the choice to leave my wife and two young children to be this person who I had finally embraced myself to be, snatching defeat from victory with reckless behavior. I thought I would break into a million pieces. I was living in the new millennia with the fear I learned in the 80s. I simply didn't know what to do. My fear of rejection was now as powerful as my fear of failure, and it was crippling.

I tried to live my truth in a way that left nobody out or sad. I planned to fall in love with a man, run the business, raise a non-traditional family, and everyone would see this as possible. I used to be incredibly capable, and now it all just sounded ridiculous. The truth was that I had been traumatized by the diagnosis and was operating in fear. I had reverted back to the child who desperately wanted to be loved and was doing every-thing possible to feel safe.

My ex-wife and I recently spoke of this challenging time in our lives as I prepared to write about it. Our conversation revealed that I had blocked from my memory a lot of what happened near the end of our marriage. So much so that her account of it all left me speechless. My recollection and the explanation I had shared with many over the years was not at all like hers. It was a much cleaner version that still held me accountable for some but not all of my actions. To hear it felt like a bad dream. I could feel her pain and sorrow as she told me her version of it.

At first, I tried to accept it all with a neutral face, but clearly, I was in shock. Her eyes went wide as she paused and said, "Don't you remember any of this?" I was silent, and I felt like a lost child in front of her. She looked at me sadly and shook her head. The damage that experience had cost us both was far greater than either of us had realized. We were both searching for answers we would never get and watching ourselves struggle with the other's recollection was disheartening. We couldn't connect all the dots, nor could we comfort each other. It was my fault. I had disassociated from it all and left her to deal with the realities of my delusions. Our marriage seemed to just end for me, but for her, we remained unresolved.

The rest of the story

My mother would listen to talk radio in the car. No matter where we went or for how long we would drive, all I heard the entire time were people talking. They'd talk about this, talk about that, and then they'd talk about this and that again. I didn't like it and I would complain except for this one man who captivated me every time he came on the radio. His name was Paul Harvey.

Paul was an American radio broadcaster known for his dramatic delivery of news stories with tactical pauses, quirky intonations, and a signature way leading into and out of a story. Paul Harvey would take you on a masterful ride, stimulating your imagination and filling your mind with thoughts and images of history, art, science, and so much more. Even though I knew there would be a climactic reveal at the end, I would not try to solve the mystery of the tale. Instead, I let him guide me masterfully to the astonishing finish.

Paul's most famous sign-off came immediately after the big reveal. He would pause, letting your mind catch up and survey the puzzle you had been assembling in your mind. After handing you the final piece, the pause would allow you to lift your head from the finished work and see the entire magnificent picture he had created with words. As you smiled in amazement, he would sign off with, "And now you know—the rest of the story."

I began writing this book at a retreat in November of 2018. It was nearly finished by Christmas, and I thought all I needed was a few dates and details my family would be able to provide. I was a little worried that sharing some of the story with them would spark conversations that might influence my writing, so I was careful who I asked. The relationship with my stepfather was challenging at best. I had worked hard to grow and forgive, remembering as many of the good things from my childhood as I could to make sure I wasn't writing from a victim's perspective. I deliberately chose not to ask my brother Mick about this chapter focusing on our stepfather.

Chuck was a good man to me. All of a sudden, the house was organized. There were rules and processes. I think I was happy to go along with them. We had new bicycles, a train set, a ski boat, and we went on many camping trips as a family together. My mother loved him and got the attention she finally deserved, but everyone else in the family did not like him. They fought him every chance they had, making fun of him and everything about him. I'm sure they were being loyal to my father, but my mother deserved their loyalty, too. I would have never known to dislike him if they had not painted him in such a bad light.

*I felt safe and taken care of, and for that, I was made to feel
like a traitor to my father and my name.*

Just one month after beginning this book, my brother Mick
called. I was hesitant to pick up because most of our conversations turned to things in our past that I didn't connect with
and certainly didn't want to bring up in conversation. I would
become anxious around him, and the intensity of that discomfort
had increased over the past two years as he struggled with his
recovery, and I struggled with my marriage. It was Christmas, he
was coming up on a year of sobriety, and I was living my truth
and taking command of my own life, so I picked up the phone.

Mick said he had came home early from football practice
that day because he had gotten injured. It was odd to have the
house open and so quiet as he made his way up the stairs to his
room. He called my name repeatedly before finding me lying face
down on the bed with my underwear halfway down my legs. My
arms were stretched out to my sides with handprints all over my
body. I'm Irish with pale skin that is sensitive to any touch. He
described other things, too, but I was just beginning to physically
experience the first part of the story. He said I was catatonic and
did not respond to him. Then he said he just snapped, knowing
what had happened and who had done it to me.

He said he began to yell for my stepfather, cussing and throw-
ing doors open to find him. When he got his hands on him, he
physically dragged my stepfather down the stairs. I had seen my
big brother unleash on Marky and put an entire bus full of kids
in shock after an older boy grabbed my shirt and told me to
give up my seat. I can only imagine what he was capable of after
finding me on that bed.

My elbows were on my knees now, one hand holding the
phone to my right ear and the other hand over my left as he
described what happened next. His words seemed to set off a fire
alarm in my body, and I winced as I began to rock forward and
backward holding my head.

The pitch was high and ripped through my brain, partially drowning out my brother's voice as images of the assault began to fill my mind. I was sweating now, and my heart felt like it was going to jump out of my chest. I rocked back and forth, picturing every word coming out of his mouth. I was fully aware of what was happening to my body and could feel everything intensify with each unbelievable image. I knew I could be anxious, hotheaded, and impatient enough to fire up my body like this, but I hadn't been any of those things when I picked up the phone. Suddenly, the feelings paired with the visions, and in that moment, I realized this life-long physiological response had connected to its source.

I could hear my stepfather breathing. Next came the smell, and finally, the feel of it all. Where did this come from? It all rolled over me like a heavy ocean wave, tossing me around under the water before dragging my flesh along the sharp rocks of the shore. I felt like I needed to catch my breath as a thought settled in my mind, *This really happened.*

"I broke his hand and some teeth as I beat him into the carpet at the bottom of the stairs," my brother said. I pictured that for a second before I was pulled back to the room where I was lying face down on the zigzag blue-and-white-patterned afghan covering the bed. I could smell the rain through the open window. I saw my arm stretched out beside me toward the dresser. It was red with handprints and appeared to be moving, but it wasn't, the rest of me was.

The police came and took my stepfather away from the house. Mick told the town sheriff what had happened, leaving out the sexual part. My mother came home soon after the police arrived, and he told her the same story. My stepfather had gone too far this time, and my brother had had enough.

I began to remember my stepfather wearing a cast on his forearm and my mother complaining about the large dental bill. I didn't know if I wanted to believe him or just let it go as another one of his embellishments. I couldn't process what I had just experienced, so despite the bed, the cast, the teeth, and my current physical response, I chose to doubt him. I'm not surprised;

it's what I knew how to do. I shook the vision out of my head and stood up to take command of the conversation. I started to pace as I waited for a moment to interrupt him. I was going to remind him what strength was. I was tired of his fucking stories of abuse and love and protection for some weak little boy!

I asked him, "Who took me to the hospital?"

He said, "Nobody, I cleaned you up and put you to bed like I always did."

I shook my head. He was filling my imagination with another one of his delusions to elevate him above his failures. He was taking advantage of me letting him close and sharing with him. I knew if I gave him an inch, he would take a mile. This is what I get for sharing and opening up. This is what I get for answering the phone!

I asked, "Why didn't you tell Mom what he supposedly did to me?"

He paused and then said, "Because I didn't want her to know it was happening to me, too."

I stopped pacing.

It was quiet for a bit. *What do I do with that?* I thought to myself. He said he wanted to tell the sheriff the whole truth, but he was ashamed of what had happened to us. Our mom was angry and confused and began to confront the sheriff. Mick said the sheriff looked him in the eye, paused for a second, placing his hand on his shoulder, and then turned to our mother and said, "Ma'am, sometimes things just have to be done." There was another long pause and then Mick said, "And that was the end of it."

A heat of rage welled up in my body as those words came out of his mouth. I started to pace my living room. *THE END OF IT!* I thought as these words began to form in my head. Fucking predators! This is what you do when you sense weakness. You take and take and take and then you take some more! The sick neighbor boy, my monster of a stepfather, and my fucking, manipulating ex-husband! I HATE YOU ALL! And you, my brother, always making up stories! You lie! You're lying to me right now! You just want to feel special and be someone close to me, but I'm not buying what you are selling anymore. None of you! You're all weak and vulnerable! YOU'RE EVERYTING I'M NOT! I won't be DEFENSLESS AGAINST THESE MONSTERS ANYMORE!

And there it was.

Not what you might think because I didn't say those words to my brother, nor did I blame him. I didn't even know it happened but buried deep down with this memory was a fear that I too would succumb to addiction and then neither of us could protect me.

He had just reached a year of sobriety; in fact, that's why I answered the call. Normally, I would let it go to voicemail so I could read the lengthy transcript instead of listening to what I considered the need in his voice. He always seemed desperate seeking acknowledgement, and telling me how much he loved me over and over again. I was incredibly insensitive and uncomfortable with it. I didn't want to be that important, loved or needed by him or anyone else. I didn't want the responsibility. What was wrong with me? Why did he evoke such emotion? I just wanted my big brother to be stronger, and when I couldn't figure out how to make him stronger, I showed him how strong I was. When that didn't work, I put distance between us.

We were both quiet now. I felt like I had been deceived, but by whom? My brother broke the silence asking, "You don't remember any of this?"

"No" I said, and then another heartbreaking realization. He thought I had and blamed him all these years, punishing him for failing to protect me from that monster. He had carried that cross for thirty-eight years. Every dismissal, every withdrawal, and every comment I made added to that heavy burden.

After that phone call with my brother, I stepped away from the book. It was near completion but had been written from a very different perspective. I was so proud of that story and felt I had grown so much in the process. I had this vision of helping my LGBTQ+ community and believed that sharing my experiences would inspire families, friends, and allies to focus on their role in developing our youth. Now, I was having visions of the assault, night terrors and insomnia. I was going to the gym twice a day to occupy my mind and getting upset every time I went back to the book.

I'd see people and they would ask me how the book was coming. I was beginning to wish I had never written it! I'd say I was writing or editing or working on a new part and they would say, "That's what you said last time." I would feel defeated and did not want to tell them the truth about what I had recently remembered and needed to process to move forward.

I was sexually assaulted thirty-seven years ago and just beginning to feel and process it for the first time. I was hurt, confused and often beside myself trying to understand how I was capable of suppressing it all. I fought to find the memories then wished I hadn't. I questioned everything. I felt broken and didn't know what was true and what was a lie. How could I lead others to their truth if I didn't even know my own? I could hear Paul Harvey's voice in my head, "Well Todd, now that you know—the rest of the story, how will you tell the rest of *this* story?" The answer was, I didn't know.

Finding my voice
and purpose

I took a spontaneous trip to Amsterdam over the New Year by myself. I walked the canals and tried to put it all together. I had come so far in my writing and battled myself to stay with it. I admit, giving up was an option but I settled on celebrating what I had achieved with some much-needed self-love. At the stroke of midnight, I set my intention that I would surrender the book and the pain to God. My focus for the next year would be to heal, and in doing so, allow myself to just be.

In mid-January, I received a call from a media agency that specialized in turning your book into a talk and helped you share your message with others. I was not interested, but the agent on the phone said she heard about my topic from a referral and asked if I would share a bit of it with her. So I did. She was moved by my story and said I should consider the good that it would do if shared with others.

I told her that some experiences in my past were recently revealed to me and that I didn't have a good grasp on what I was supposed to do next. I went on to say that I had begun to seek counseling from the Veteran's Administration for what was most likely Post-Traumatic Stress Disorder or PTSD. I said I thought it a good idea to detach from the story, that I was not interested, and just needed to let it go. It was bad enough that I had been talking about it to my family and friends as well as connecting with local LGBTQ+ organization for resources and support. She understood and asked if she could share what we talked about with a colleague and if I'd take a call from her if she discovered anything that might help get me back on track. I said sure just to end the call, and that seemed to be the end of it.

The next day I received a call from Kristen White of White Media Agency. We talked for quite some time, and she suggested that creating a talk and filming it might be the best way to work through the emotion and help me find the real message in my story. I believed in what I was doing, but I was afraid to dig any deeper. She persisted, and I felt she was sincere, so I agreed.

Over the next two months, I dug deep and pulled the message out of the book, finding my voice and purpose. The talk was beautiful, and when I watched it for the first time, I cried. I knew it needed to be shared. I watched it over and over to remind me that I had value, and with a renewed sense of purpose and courage, I began writing again.

I went back to this book, and despite it being written with the knowledge I had at the time, it was no longer my truth. So much of it needed to be changed. I struggled with new discoveries as memories steadily appeared from my past. I continued to be treated for PTSD, and that created even more problems as I unpacked my emotional baggage attached to nearly every significant life experience after the age of twelve. It was intellectually challenging, emotionally draining, and spiritually revealing. I remained an open wound, afraid and uncomfortable with this new knowledge and the words it produced as I wove the truth into in this story.

Cycle of self-abuse

Counseling was intense and revealing as I become aware of how I responded to stress. I began a treatment called Eye Movement Desensitization and Reprocessing (EMDR). It is a psychotherapy treatment designed to alleviate the distress associated with traumatic memories. It's necessary for patients to acknowledge stressful situations to become aware of how and why they respond. To do so, you need to connect with these experiences to reprogram the mind and create new behaviors.

I began to notice things I did throughout my life to avoid and cope and then connect them to thoughts and feelings. I would count or repeat a phrase over and over in my mind as I watched scenarios play out in my head, often surprised at the amount of time that would pass. Ruminating is associated with anxiety and depression that focuses on inadequacy and worthlessness. I would count to five using my fingers and thumb or slightly tap my teeth as the numbers passed through my mind. The fan blades were a common focus. I'd struggle to get out of bed and look up to watch them spin as I counted all five, occasionally fixing on one and watching it go around and around as my mind searched for a reason to get out of bed.

I don't know when the cycle of self-abuse started but I can tell you I have always been critical of myself and afraid of failing. This intensified with age and experience, the greater the challenge the bigger the need to cope. I thought it was all related to my big gay secret, and for the longest time, it was. Once I became sexually active as a gay man, the suppressed experiences with male predators began to do their damage, polluting and sabotaging nearly every experience. I rationalized it was my sexual culture, desires, or my partner's wants and needs, so therefore it wasn't abuse, it was my choice.

I sought counseling over the years to address the guilt associated with abandoning my family and shame associated with getting HIV but never considered an unhealthy emotional and physical connection to sex. It didn't exist, and therefore, I didn't think to seek help for it. Knowing what it took to address it now leads me to believe I chose to ignore it because to admit a problem was accepting weakness and lack of control. That core deficiency of mine could never be denied.

I believed that coming out was the solution to all my problems. To think I could simply change my sexual partners to men and be happy was naive. I didn't have a chance to develop any skills or learn any healthy lessons as a gay man before getting infected. I was traumatized by the diagnosis immediately after experiencing the euphoria of my truth. I was still hiding, still lying, and ultimately, still coping. To make matters worse, the sexual trauma was now working full-time in the background to amplify my shame and fear with every triggering experience.

Proclaiming your sexual identity is empowering and important to release associated guilt and shame. It is also necessary to begin living your truth in a healthy way. I had not released it because I didn't know it existed, and so the cycle of abuse continued with me as the abuser.

I had learned that failure and weakness were punishable. I was incredibly thorough and tenacious at it. I set my own expectations so high that they could only be attainable with suffering. Nobody really expected that from me, but then again, how did I know. I believed that whatever was asked of me was expected of me.

I was incredibly insecure, and I would project so much confidence that I would fool myself. I needed to feel that way, and when people called me arrogant, I felt the need to work even harder because everyone wants the arrogant guy to fail. I was a scared little boy putting on his best face, and if I didn't deliver, everything would crumble, and I'd be exposed.

I would create a goal and attack it like a mission. The energy expended to operate at such a high level for extended periods of time could not be sustained. I was at DEFCON 2 for as long as my body and mind could handle it. Once exhausted and anticipating failure, I would unravel, isolate, and abuse myself again and again. It was a never-ending cycle.

Coworkers, friends, and my lover became my enemies. It would begin with anxiety and work its way to conflict and ultimately a dramatic, destructive conclusion. Abandonment or betrayal were my go-to reasons. I thought that by defeating others, I would fix accountability on them, and escape responsibility and shame. After all, this little boy needed love, acceptance, and admiration, and you don't get those things when you're a failure. You get stripped down in front of people, publicly shamed, and then beaten.

Desires far exceed
our experience

Coming out was not the end of the game of hide and seek for me. I wasn't instantly liberated, transformed, or even safe. In fact, the game became more complex because it was never just about being gay. It's never is just one thing. It's a culmination of things, and many heterosexuals play a huge role in creating difficulties for LGBTQ+ people with hurtful words and actions.

I didn't know where to seek men like me other than bars, and those were not the best choices, but how would I know? I had begun hiding at a very young age, and although I came out at thirty-two, I felt like an awkward adolescent again. I lacked experience and the emotional resources of family and friends. I had isolated myself and worked overtime to hide my sexual identity and desires. I wanted to believe I was bisexual; it seemed like a reasonable and somewhat acceptable solution. I was "kind of" gay, so maybe I would be accepted with all my heterosexual accomplishments as if they were somehow associated with my sexuality. If that were true, they would carry weight when I was judged.

Most of what I learned about my sexuality was self-taught. There wasn't a Homo 101 course or elective to take when I was in college, and there was no way I'd walk in that classroom anyway. And like many of us, our desires far exceed our experience and knowledge, making us prey for those who would take advantage of us, heterosexual or otherwise. You would be one of the lucky ones if you were actually ready, willing, and emotionally able to participate in your first same-sex encounter. Most of us are not that fortunate, and these experiences impact us mentally, physically, spiritually, and emotionally.

Dating and hookup apps can be unhealthy, too. We can develop habits and associations with these instant gratifying experiences and fail to develop the discipline and intimacy necessary for healthy relationships. You can rationalize that its easy and convenient, but if it is simply for sex and you are hoping for lightning to strike, you better be grounded in who you are, or you'll continue to be shocked at what you find in these encounters.

Exaggerated profiles, face-tuned photos, multiple profiles, and carefully constructed personalities make it too easy to lose your integrity and identity online. And when we ultimately meet people in person with whom we've interacted with online, the discrepancies create frustration and mistrust. Our disappointments are so great and so frequent that when we do find someone we like, we are willing to turn a simple "hello" into "I do" because our standards are so low. It's only a matter of time before we lose the ability to interact with integrity because we will have lost our truth in the editing.

PART 6

Dad

A conversationalist is someone who is good at or enjoys engaging in conversations with others. I don't know that I enjoyed speaking with people, but I was good at it. I've always been more comfortable eliciting emotional responses than expressing my own feelings. Avoiding and hiding my emotions is something I have deliberately worked at and believed I had perfected over the years. This attempt at control made me feel safe, enjoying one-sided connections with others requiring little emotional investment on my part.

The military provided yet another stereotypical environment to hide my insecurity and secret. When necessary, I could be direct, void of emotion and sarcastic in my dealings with others, even my family. I began to feel more comfortable engaging with people because I could just as easily disengage with them if I became unsettled. The problem with being one-sided is that there really isn't a connection. Relationships and conversations require at least two participants, or the entire exchange is just one person talking at another. This practice may have initially helped with the fear of being vulnerable to others but evolved into a dysfunctional habit of being emotionally unavailable, particularly when I was wrong.

A good sense of humor also helped keep interactions from getting too personal. It's easy to influence the direction of conversation with humor. A laugh is seldom denied, and most people welcome humor to lighten a heavy conversation or create a break just long enough for you to exit. I refer to this technique at the "parting shot."

My father was a master of the parting shot. A brilliant conversationalist and relatable man, he traveled the world selling his products by first selling himself. "Son, life is all about people and the relationships you have with them," he would say. He was also incredibly charming and seemed to influence anyone he exchanged words with, especially me.

Dad spoke with everyone about anything and everything. He found people and their stories fascinating. One of his favorite words to say was "interesting," and when he said it, he meant it. The inflection in his voice and the look in his eyes revealed it. It was effortless for him to begin conversations organically and then guide them toward a purpose, pacing and leading those around him with skill and precision. It was beautiful to watch him navigate a situation and even more exciting to be a part of it.

During our travels, we would end most days in a hotel room with a drink and conversation. Regardless of my perception of the day, dad always pointed out the successes, no matter how small. It served no one to focus on the negative, even if it involved the loss of money.

This optimism required him to carefully choose words that acknowledged the loss and celebrated the win. I didn't always understand the value in this practice, and at first, I thought he was just selling the idea that we didn't fail that day. Instead, he was deliberately staying focused and optimistic to keep our energy and spirits up. This helped him acknowledged his fear of failure and to speak his faith in "the Man upstairs" as he called Him to provide new opportunities and breath in his lungs to make the most of them. I'm grateful to have shared these moments with him. He was incredibly complex and difficult to read at times, but I connected with that and even found it comforting.

On one particular evening, we settled in for a talk with a couple extra mini-bottles of scotch that he managed to get from the flight attendant after their brief conversation on the plane earlier that day. I commented about it as he handed me one of the bottles. It was sarcastic, unnecessary, and I could tell he didn't feel comfortable with what I said. It was uncharacteristic of me and sounded like something you'd hear in a men's locker room. It didn't even feel good to hear myself say it.

He smiled halfheartedly as he passed me a glass of ice and asked me what I thought it meant to be charming. I paused for a second, and despite his reaction to my initial chauvinistic comment, I went all-in with more masculine themes and language that took the conversation in a direction I didn't plan for it to go. I couldn't stop myself. I could hear myself sounding even more ridiculous and began to panic. I tried every tactic I knew to bring the rant to a conclusion but got nothing from him. Not a smile, a nod, or even a grunt. He just sat there contemplatively staring into his scotch while slowly stirring it with his finger.

I began to sweat as I rambled on, feeling more and more uncomfortable with the situation. It reminded of a similar experience I had in the Army as a young second lieutenant. I was giving a tactical briefing to a senior officer and lost my train of thought. In a panic, I began to ramble on and on until it became obvious to everyone, including myself, that I had no idea what I was talking about. Finally, the senior officer put his hand up in the air, signaling me to stop and command everyone's attention. He then said, "Lieutenant, when you find yourself in a hole, do yourself a favor and stop digging." Ugh, I can still feel that moment.

Finally, aware that I was deep into a similar lesson, I stopped talking and took a deep breath. Dad took a sip of scotch, looked at me with sincerity, and said, "To be charming is to have a genuine interest in others." He went on to explain that he didn't ask the flight attendant for the mini-bottles of scotch and that the conversation began because he noticed her Midwestern accent. I assumed he was charming her, flirting, and manipulating her for something. That's what we do when we don't know any better. We follow the examples we see in movies, locker rooms, and beer commercials. Not only was I wrong, but I had also offended him. He didn't want me to think of him that way, regardless of what I had heard growing up.

He admitted to deliberately being unresponsive while I "ran my mouth." He actually said it was funny to watch me dig myself a grave and that I sounded immature and inexperienced, both of which he said were not true, making sure my self-esteem remained intact. This was something I came to love most about my dad. He never seemed to take pleasure in being right, only in making me better.

We talked some more and laughed as he shared all the times he had dug himself into holes and the colorful lessons he learned from the experiences. He mixed humility, humor, and creativity in the most beautiful way to make my lessons easy to experience and learn from, just like he did with the letters outside the post office twenty-five years earlier. He didn't always practice what he preached, but he did often enough to earn my loyalty. He was mindful of the influence I gave him in my life and took care to do what he hadn't for so long—teach me.

I had never known anyone as in tune with his surrounding as I was. I could feel him thinking, and we shared as much time talking as we did in silence. It didn't make sense to many that this complex and dynamic person could disconnect for hours, even days at a time. Except for the evening news, there was no need for any more noise than what was already in his head.

One of his favorite things to do was mow the five acres of grass that blanketed the rolling slopes and wrapped around the tall walnut trees surrounding his Iowa home. To most, it would seem like a horrible chore, but to him, a magnificent gift combining many of his favorite things—work, challenge, solace, and nature.

I don't listen to music in my car or watch television in my home. My left ear constantly rings, and on occasion, my right chimes in for a surround-sound effect. I don't mind it. When I sleep, I lay on my right side, and it's like having a sleep machine to drown out remaining noise created by the slight imbalance of the fan above my bed.

Being okay with yourself and being alone is an art. It takes discipline and practice to concentrate at that level. It's not unlike meditation. You're incredibly mindful and connected to yourself and whatever you are focusing on. However, I'd like to think I had always practiced this discipline, but I'm sure much of it was isolation. When caught off-guard in this state of mind with the wrong sort of inquiry, it would elicit a damaging response from me. I feared failure and looking incapable, so if I was caught off-guard, I would panic and express myself in unproductive ways.

I learned not to come at my father in this way, either. I believe he wanted to look good in my eyes just as much as I wanted to impress him, and if I appeared to be critical or disrespectful, he would react similarly. Although he would catch himself quickly, I recognized the behavior in him. Of course, he would respond that way. Like me, he took pride in being prepared. After he composed himself, he'd remind me that I needed to choose my words carefully if I expected others to do the same for me.

He was incredibly proud of me and went out of his way to let me and others know how he felt. I loved and respected my father and feel even more connected to him since his death. He made a lot of choices in his life that had adversely affected us as a family, but that is the nature of choices. Except for one incredibly confusing and frightening time in our relationship, my faith in him remained unshaken. I didn't have the emotional or intellectual maturity as a child to fully understand those choices, but as an adult, I most certainly can choose how they affect me now. Make a choice, learn from it, and then make your next best choice.

After his death, I reflected on our relationship. Words matter a great deal to me, and although I could not say that I trusted my father, I can say with conviction that I believed in him. I think I loved him more because he was so fallible, and when he let his guard down, there was a vulnerability I connected with.

I wonder what it was like to be him as a child. What shaped him, guided him, and drove him? Maybe he was afraid, just like me. Maybe he felt that giving energy to fault or weakness threatened the image he created to hide his shortcomings and shame. I believe he operated on high alert, too, struggling with the secrets he kept, promises he made, and expectations he set—all his own doing, just like mine. No one told him to be successful, better, or more of anything. It was simply who he was.

If those expectations were based in fear, there was no truth in them because, in my eyes, he was a giant. I didn't see weakness in him, nor did I look, but I kept a critical eye on myself for half a century. The fear of him not loving me was one of the first I realized held no truth. He never said I should be successful. Instead, he said I should deliver on my word. "Do the work, son, and the money will come."

In essence, he was saying I *was* enough, and all I needed to do was apply myself. People saw my father as arrogant at times, but I saw passion, confidence, and determination. Where others saw a man putting on a show, I saw a man who *was* the show, and despite all our faults and failings, he gave me hope.

Daddy

People ask, "How did you raise such amazing children?" I'd just smile to acknowledge the compliment, never letting it land with me. The truth is that I didn't, she did. I literally did what she taught me to do, suggested I do, and most importantly, what they needed me to do.

"She" is the mother of our children and one of the most important people in my life. Our story is complexly beautiful, and to tell it from my perspective will not do it justice. You'll have to wait for Jennifer to share it. For now, simply know that she is an angel, and without her love and resiliency, our unique family would not have survived.

I was emotionally detaching from them well before the end of our marriage. The preoccupation with being gay, finding my truth, and protecting my reputation made me emotionally inaccessible. It's easy for me to write *with* emotion but challenging to write *about* my emotions.

I didn't understand this when I began to write this book. I'd stare at one sentence in a single paragraph and ruminate about it for hours. I would get angry at myself and question if the point I was trying to make was relevant and at times, even true. I've always been this way despite suppressing my thoughts and feelings for so long. Having said that, you'd think they would pour out of me, but like everything else, I needed them to be just right, to be perfect. I realize now it wasn't the words themselves, it was the truth in them.

I've made so many choices that have caused others pain that I struggle with the regret. The most troubling was the choice to live my life as a gay man after committing to living it as a heterosexual man with a family. I'm mostly at peace with it now, but for nearly twenty years, I've drowned in the guilt associated with leaving my wife and children.

I was just seven years old when my father left under "normal" circumstances, and here I was coming out with my son at the same age. Not only was I leaving, but I also wasn't even the person they thought me to be. Okay, I know now that's not entirely true, but I did say I was *mostly* at peace with it. Staying connected physically and emotionally was terribly difficult. I couldn't connect with that shame, nor could I ignore what they were feeling. They were confused and afraid, and so was I.

My son is the most inquisitive and determined child I've ever met. He challenged me with everything necessary to become an exceptional father, and just when I thought I'd got the hang of it, he'd push my skills and imagination to a new level. The questions this kid asked were incredibly well thought out. You could not ignore him, brush him off, or talk at him. To converse with him left me smiling in amazement or grimacing with frustration. He was tireless, relentless, and truly extraordinary.

U.S. Army Regulations guiding the wear and appearance of the uniform were clear, none more so observed or obvious than the wearing of a cover, a hat. Simply put, if you do not have a hat on, you are out of uniform and cannot be outside. Except when in physical fitness attire and not directed to wear a stocking cap because of the cold temperatures, a soldier must always cover their head when outside. It was as if God himself would make a fist and strike down from heaven pounding your undisciplined, coverless body into the ground like a tent spike should you violate his eleventh commandment. After which, your fellow service members would cover the bloody spot on the ground with the appropriate hat for the uniform you were just driven to rest in, thereby restoring order to the universe.

My brilliant son deduced that a lack of cover was like house arrest for me. It didn't matter the time of day, uniform of choice, or mission assigned, no hat meant I could not leave, and he made it a priority to hide it every chance he got.

His active mind made it difficult for him to rest, and I would wake up on countless occasions with him standing at my bedside just inches from my face whispering, "Daddy? Hey, Daddy."

It would scare the crap out of me. Slightly terrorized, greatly confused, and completely irritated, I would respond, "Yes, son?"

He would say something like, "Tomorrow, can we try to beat the boss again on Legend of Zelda?"

I'd reply, "Yes, son. Now go to bed."

He would smile and giggle with excitement stating, "I know we're going to get him this time, right, Daddy?"

"Yes, son," I'd reply. "Now get to bed; Daddy has to get up in two hours."

"Okay, Daddy. I love you." Then he'd smile, kiss me, and walk slowly back to his room where he no doubt played the video game battle with the "boss" over and over again in his head until he'd fall asleep from mental exhaustion.

The morning would come, and I'd slip out of the house in the dark for physical training and return a little over an hour later. I'd shower, eat, and then get dressed in my Battle Dress Uniform (BDU). I didn't have much time, but it was enough to be with them at the beginning of each day, and that was important. He was always just a few feet away from me, scaling the doorways with his hands and clammy feet. He would sit on the bed with a book or game at the ready should he find an opportunity to decisively engage me in conversation.

In military terms, to be "decisively engaged" is to have lost your ability to maneuver or break contact with an opposing force. In the event either force does not break contact, they must battle it out until someone wins. In other words, if I got into a conversation with my son before work, it would ultimately end in tears or me making promises I could not keep, leading to more tears that evening.

Anxiety would build as the time for me to leave approached, but I'd do my best to appease him. He was really good at getting me to commit to every minute that remained in the day beginning the second I got home. I know this seems incredibly complex for a four-year-old, but I want to do justice to the creativity with which this child expressed his love and desire for my attention.

I must admit, despite the frustration and anxiety it caused us both, to engage in this intellectual dual with my son was one of the highlights of my day. And like my father, the determination and imagination he used to pace and lead me to his desired outcome was remarkable. It was beautiful to watch him navigate each scenario and even more exciting to be a part of it.
Ultimately, I knew it all came down to me finding the hat, making concessions, and leaving for work. Being the adult in the scenario meant it was my ultimate responsibility to ensure I left him in a healthy state so his mother would not lose her mind cleaning up the mess after our morning exchange.

He would start with, "What time do you get home from work tonight, Daddy?"

And, "How long do you think it will take for you to eat your dinner?"

I'd attempt to reply, "Well, I'm…"

He would cut me off mid answer to follow though with his thought, "Wait a minute, Daddy, I'll go ask Mommy what we're having for dinner so you can answer for real, okay?"

I couldn't help but begin to smile as I said, "Okay, son." As he ran to the kitchen.

He'd look back, hold up a one finger indicating he'd be right back as he stated, "Hold on, okay, Daddy? Stay right here; I'll be right back!"

Off he would scamper into the kitchen and return with details of our evening dinner, and then he would continue with, "Last night, we were done by 7:15, Daddy, so do you think we can be done by 7:15 again, Daddy?"

I'd smile and say, "I suppose so."

He'd follow me around the house as I searched for my hat. "What are you looking for, Daddy?" he'd say, pretending to look with me. Getting down and looking under the couch, behind the grandfather clock, or in the cushion of my green reclining chair.

"My hat, son." I'd say. I'd look a couple different places before I could no longer play the game and then look to his mother to see if I had given sufficient effort. If I got a smile, I'd pretend to find a spare hidden in the cargo pocket of my BDU pants or duty bag. "Well, I guess I'll have to wear my spare today" I'd say, and then give him a hug, thanking him for helping me search for my hat. He would fight back the tears as I promised a number of things we would do together when I got home. I'd pick him up and hug him and tell him I loved him. He would nearly break my neck with his hug. I miss that.

"Hurry home, Daddy," he'd say through his teary-eyed smile, and off I'd go to work.

If the average child is perceptive, what was my son? I believe he felt my reservation, and like no one else, sensed that I wasn't always present. I was the same age when my father chose to leave, and all I can remember was feeling left behind. I came out, changed everything, got infected, and immediately went back into hiding, all in just forty-five days. I can understand my instinct to survive and the energy it consumed, but the reality is that I failed to consider how they would feel when I revealed this additional truth.

Hey, "Daddy"

Daddy meant something very different in my new lifestyle. In gay culture, it is used to describe an older gay man sexually involved in a relationship with a younger gay man. The difference in age may vary, but the relationship can feel like a traditional son-father dynamic with the younger seeking guidance and support in a number of ways from the older. If both are comfortable in their roles, they can give and receive to meet each other's needs, enjoying a healthy and fulfilling relationship. On the other hand, the relationship may be the backdrop for unresolved issues of a male child and his father to be played out in unhealthy behavior as an adult.

"Gay daddy issues" is a term used for psychological challenges stemming from an absent or dysfunctional relationship with one's father. This manifests itself in trust issues of both self and others, a need to please, sexual desire for older men who act like fathers, and a number of other issues related to esteem and insecurity.

The sex itself doesn't always mirror the social, financial, or even physical aspects of the relationship. In fact, it can be very different, depending on the desires of each partner.

With age can come energy, patience, and performance challenges for the older partner with the younger typically having more energy, less stress, and a strong desire for social activities. Youth seldom has the advantage with intimacy because it is so much more rewarding when it goes beyond the physical. Younger partners can be inexperienced, immature, inhibited, and insecure. Don't get offended too soon, boys, because daddies can be all those things as well.

The fear of getting older and losing the younger man or getting older and losing the *older* man may linger in the back of either partner's minds. These insecurities are present in most relationships, homosexual or otherwise, and unless they are addressed, the union will suffer and possibly fail. Doubts about the other's intentions enter into the relationship space and can take over conversations.

This is a serious challenge for many in the LGBTQ+ community. With little to no successful relationship experience or communication skills to handle conflict, they must figure it out on their own. At best, the more mature partner can facilitate the conversation, coaching, and guiding the younger to a healthy resolution. Or, he could just as easily seize the upper hand as the younger partner grapples with confidence and self-worth. In the absence of experience, the younger can easily resort to emotional manipulation and passive-aggressive behavior aimed at the insecurities of the older.

I personally struggle with any relationship that functions with an element of control. The idea that you have to give to get supports that everything has a price and that nothing, even love, is unconditional. The younger can usually relate because it wasn't long ago that they had a similar understanding with their own parents, and oh, by the way, wouldn't it be nice to have the security and resources of my parents with freedom, access, and the sex I desire? Let's not forget the daddy and his wish always to have the financial upper hand in a relationship and be able to do and get what he wants, when and how he wants it, including sex with a younger man. There is a steep learning curve in every relationship, but the power dynamic created by the daddy-son pairing is tricky and can quickly shift from mutual respect and guidance to contempt and neglect.

The negative stereotype of this coupling in our community is very strong. Even couples who seem to make it work find themselves defending the integrity of their relationship as they experience disapproving looks and derogatory comments. Then, there are those who brag about their arrangement with objectifying comments about the boy or displaying gifts given by the daddy. To each their own, but consenting adults deserve the opportunity to love one another in a safe and supportive environment, and we should discourage behavior that erodes the integrity of our community by disrespecting any segment of it. In the end, only we know what is true in our hearts, and if its love, we should choose to honor it.

Being alone scares people, particularly when it comes to getting older. Waiting too long to decide what you want in life and how you want to live that life seems to be a pattern in our society as a whole. In gay culture, we typically get a late start with sex and emotional development. With the freedom of our twenties and the sex drive of our teens, we enter into adulthood eager to exercise our freedom. Instead of harnessing that energy and passion toward a life plan, we run smack into the gay social scene that not only welcomes your lust but promotes and encourages it.

This can be challenging for daddy and son because the security of one and the sexual gratification of the other needs to be met, and without honest communication, most will choose safety over integrity.

It may take time to establish enough trust to display all of your sexual wants and desires, but they will eventually be expressed either through fantasy, with your partner, someone invited into the relationship, or with someone outside the relationship.

Well, that's not entirely true either. Many cannot reconcile the "ideal" relationship with the truth. The fear of disappointing your partner and the desire to experiment are at constant odds with many people, gay or otherwise. We want to have our vulnerability received and reciprocated. That's the point of real intimacy—trust. It's when the walls come down that we are able to give and receive love authentically in the most beautiful way.

Dating and sex apps provide instant gratification. This is problematic for many just coming out. The ease and frequency of sexual encounters devalues many important interpersonal skills that have value in nearly all our relationships. In addition, they provide an unhealthy way to avoid all things less appealing than sex. We linger too long in this phase, postponing our mental, spiritual, emotional, and financial growth. Our preoccupation with instant gratifying behavior distracts us from setting goals, seeking education, acquiring resources, and developing the discipline needed to get what we want—if we've taken the time even to figure that out.

There's no truth in fear

I don't know many older couples, but those I do know are incredibly proud of the individual and collective work done to make their relationships successful. Most have struggled with personal demons, culture traps, and self-sabotage, but all found a greater appreciation for each other and their relationship particularly those old enough to have lived through the AIDS epidemic.

If relationships are so hard, why do we keep trying? I think it's hard because bars and clubs and parties are hiding places, too. Every time we fail at a relationship, we head back to those hiding places to be recycled with other single people through the same system that produced our last failure. I normally don't use the word failure, but in this case, I will. It's only a failure if we *fail* to learn the lesson.

I think a better question to ask is what can we do to make healthy LGBTQ+ relationships easier to form and sustain? One answer is to get beyond the bars of shame, guilt, fear, and lies that hold us back, and the bars that perpetuate these unhealthy behaviors. I'm not saying going out to the clubs is bad; I'm saying we should ask ourselves what we're looking for and if that's the place to find it. If you just want to let off some steam and that's your truth, go for it. Just remember to build up the same amount of steam to fuel your passion and achieve your goals.

Not having role models or healthy sources to learn from remains a problem for LGBTQ+ youth. So many of us don't realize the value in our lessons and choose our fear over the progress of others. There's no truth in fear. The only failure of a poor choice is the choice to hide the lesson in the shame. Fear is a liar, and when we succumb to it, love loses. I struggle throughout this book with fear and shame, but I've learned how to identify it, acknowledge it, and then choose to make the next best choice for me and for others.

I also know many mature gay men who are happy being single and love the unique lifestyle they have created for themselves. Most admit to one key factor in their happiness—loving and accepting themselves. It's easy to get lost in the excitement of social activities that encourage freedom and expression, but if it becomes your single focus, you can wake up decades later unprepared for that future you are now in.

Most admit they would prefer a partner but now have much higher expectations then they did before they held themselves to a higher standard. Self-love, focus, worth, and self-esteem have replaced self-*ish*, and we as a culture are beginning to become self-aware. It is a hope of mine to inspire more of my generation to shed their shame and take the next step of coming out to let *out* the pain, passion, and priceless experiences their lessons have produced.

For me, I came out at thirty-two and was happy to act like a twenty-two-year-old gay man, and that meant spending time with them. In addition, I was very young looking for my age, and it seemed like a natural fit. I was making up for lost time and playing the part. What part, I was not sure of. I dated younger men for their looks and energy as well as their desire to be coached. It fed my ego to help them with life challenges they had not experienced yet. Being a father, veteran, entrepreneur, and well educated meant I had a lot to offer, but I didn't want to be a "daddy" because I already was one. Younger men were looking for attention and security, but so was I, and I didn't like to share it. I had gone without it long enough, and that created a whole new set of challenges.

Identity, self-respect and many other factors are at work here, and the hope that we can somehow manifest a healthy relationship from a lie is unrealistic. For me, it was the experiences related to my abuse. I falsely believed that because I created the opportunity and type of sexual experience that I was somehow in control of abusive behavior. Many of my issues affected what I wanted, what I thought I needed, and what I was going to get out of it. In the end, it was just me being abused all over again with the illusion that I was in control.

Lowering your inhibitions with drugs and alcohol is not uncommon for anyone avoiding pain. An altered state can allow you to push limits, let go of inhibitions, and exonerate yourself from responsibility. It's easy to go too far with a little help from substances, and many chose this option. First, it's to experiment and experience, then a habit, and eventually, an addiction.

Dangerous places to hide

It's hard to focus on the present when you are suffering and stuck in the pain of the past. Preoccupation with failure and the people, places, and experiences associated with them can make you feel less than and can keep you from moving in the direction you had planned for your life. Our routines get infected and the places we want to avoid become so many that escape can only come from running or yet another level of hiding—altered states. Alcohol and drugs are easily obtained and accepted in many social aspects of our culture. They are not for everyone but are easily found. It's a choice and dangerous places to hide. A simple change in activities or your circle of friends can connect you with many opportunities to get hurt. If you are not careful, you can be swept away and lost completely. This is where you cut your leg on the big saw behind the paneling.

Too many get caught up in it all and simply forget their priorities and responsibilities. Others forget who they are all together. I spent nearly a decade chasing the promise of fun and excitement at festivals and other events thinking that was where I would experience the fullness of being gay. The euphoria never lasted or resulted in a meaningful relationship, just the promise of another opportunity in the next city.

I was just a little boy playing a game that left a scar on my leg. Who was I before I got hurt, and who would I have become without that experience? It only matters if we stop it from happening again. For me, what is done is done, and if changing that experience as a child means losing all the beautiful gifts I've received in my life, I'll keep the scar.

PART 7

Every poor choice

I've never been a crier. I didn't like the face that went along with it, and I could never sustain the emotion. But every so often, I would be caught off-guard and begin to cry. I would get warm in the face, feel the lump in my throat, mucus in my nose and then, as if a switch were thrown, everything would just power down. Nothing remained but a tear and some snot to wipe off my face. Lately, it had been a different experience because I'd begin to cry before I woke up.

I slept on my back and way over on my side of the bed. This ensured the bed was easy to make in the morning because I seldom moved. I'd just lay there with my eyes open as I imagined every poor choice projected from my brain onto the ceiling like a movie screen. I don't like scary movies, and when forced to watch, I cover my eyes. The same was true with this feature. I'd get to a part that I couldn't watch then shift my stare to the fan blades. Counting them one through five and often grabbing just one and following it around several times before blinking and sending tears to my ears, reminding me of another time I laid perfectly still in pain. Eventually, I would fall asleep and begin next morning right where I left off.

I had turned fifty just a week before, and it had been forty-five years since that boy wounded me, and yet here I was, flat on my back, frozen in fear that seemed greater than any I could remember. Why? I'd like to say it was because of another boy, but I was running out of people to blame and places to hide.

Hmm, where was this going?

This boy and I started with clear intentions, the intention to find someone to have sex with. I think it was just a torso shot with him in jeans. It was gay.com, and I'm not even sure what his profile said. Did it really matter? The address was a house just south of the nearby university. He was twenty, going to school, had a roommate, a book bag, and his mattress was on the floor. I was thirty-eight, running a business, lived alone, carried a briefcase, and slept in a custom-made bed. Hmm, where was this going?

I was selling insurance and had a client nearby, so I said I'd meet him. His roommate answered the door looking incredibly put out by the expense of energy and loss of valuable TV time. He looked me up and down and without a single word, pointed to a room upstairs. I wondered how many times a day he pointed to that room. Anxiety set in, and for a moment, I thought about turning around and leaving, but he did have a nice body, and I was already there. I turned and closed the door behind me, briefly reconsidering the choice I had just made. "Todd?" I heard a voice say. I turned around, and the first thing I saw was his beautiful smile.

I stayed a bit after. We sat on the end of the mattress, smiling at each other. It felt a bit awkward but surprisingly good at the same time, not what I had imagined when I walked in the door. I remember sitting quietly next to each other for quite some time. We were touching from shoulder to ankle and I remember thinking that I wished I hadn't slept with him because I wanted more. He broke the silence by offering me a piece of chocolate. It seemed odd for such an occasion, but I politely accepted. I had never had anything like it before. It was beautifully wrapped in shiny gold paper resting neatly in its own pleated, paper base. I unwrapped it carefully, revealing a rich, light brown milk chocolate covering a hazelnut center. I held it in my hand as I looked at him admiring his beautiful skin, soft lips and welcoming eyes. It was sweet how he nudged me with his body, smiled and said, "Take a bite." So I did.

Over the next year and a half, we met up every so often. Always at my house, beginning with a text that would result in me leaving the door unlocked even though I had already gone to bed. He'd be in and out by dawn. He never stayed, and I never asked why. I just assumed he had somewhere to be. Later, I learned he thought I had a boyfriend, and at times I did, but not when I was with him.

We would also see each other at the club. He would be with someone and entice me, or I would dance close enough to distract him. Sometimes, I was bold and slide in between him and his date to see if he would come home with me. He did nearly every time, but when he didn't, I'd get a text and unlock the door.

I never got tired of him, and why would I? He was always ready, willing and asked nothing of me. It didn't hurt that I dreamed of being with him, dreamed of being in love with him. I think I knew exactly who he was the moment I laid eyes on him—me.

I remember asking God to give me someone just like me. I wanted to do and be all the things I had imagined when I first came out, before getting infected. I had struggled to find emotional and financial security after Jennifer and I divorced and settled into a routine that I believed allowed me to be a father and a gay man. It was something I fought hard to accomplish and believed would make me happy. It did not.

I avoided relationships and commitment, becoming more and more isolated. I was making great money and had a group of friends that I liked, but it wasn't enough, I wanted more. What I wanted was him and I began to show him by reaching out more and more. This changed the dynamic a bit. He started needing things, mostly gas money. He would be somewhere in a dramatic dilemma with a story to support it, and I'd go put some gas in his car. Other times, he would hint for things, but I wouldn't respond. I had a rule: If it's not food, gas, or medicine, you need to seek help from your family. That seemed to keep things manageable.

I learned more about his family and heard stories of abuse, abandonment, and neglect. I believed him because I saw so much of me in him. I could see he was hurt and also that he was manipulative. He did it both consciously and subconsciously, mainly with passive-aggressive behavior and guilt. Oddly enough, it just made me want him more. I knew what he needed to be happy, healthy, and whole—me. He wanted to trust me and to believe I was different from the men he shared himself with for gain. He also wanted me to trust him and was very careful not to ask for too much too soon. I wonder if he told himself it was because he really liked me or because he really wanted me to like him. I'm sure it was a bit of both because that's how I felt about him.

I played along with his games because a part of me believed we could be more together than we were separate. I thought our dysfunction could be our redemption if we could just love and trust each other. To be accountable to someone who knew exactly who I was and who would hold me to my word. Yes, I know how codependent that sounds, but stay with me here, this isn't easy to acknowledge. I would share my life experiences with him and help him get to where I was: lost—oops, I meant successful, healthy, and happy.

He was eager to let me guide him and fed my ego with his vulnerability and appreciation. He was portraying himself to be a wounded bird, and I thought that because I knew what he was doing, I wasn't being manipulated. He didn't care or probably consider that I loved him and believed he was worth the risk, he just wanted me to take the risk.

The most absurd story!

He was younger, but we were both emotionally immature, and it was only a matter of time before we tested the happiness we couldn't possibly deserve. One day, he called me, stating he was in Wisconsin or somewhere in the middle of the country. He said he had to go back to see family on short notice and could only afford a one-way ticket and needed help to get home to go to school and work. I suggested he ask his family for assistance. He said they wouldn't help and actually made him feel horrible for even asking them for help.

He went on and on about getting paid and how his roommate owed him money and other things. He begged, and I wanted to believe him. It was $345, and I made him promise to pay me back by the end of the week. He agreed, and I wired the money. Oddly enough, I felt really good about helping him. That was a big thing for me to do, and it felt like he trusted me enough to call, and I trusted him enough to help. In my mind, this was a step closer together, and I felt really good about it. I felt so good that I called my mother and told her I had met someone.

A couple days went by, and I called to make sure he got home safely, but he didn't answer. I left a voicemail and thought little of it. Several days passed, and I began to leave more voicemails. First concern, then disappointment, and finally anger. After a week of frustration, it occurred to me that something happened. Maybe he lost his phone, couldn't pay his bill, or worse, he was actually hurt. I left another message, apologizing, and expressed that I hope he wasn't hurt. Soon, his voice mailbox was full, and I was left wondering if he played me or if something happened.

Ultimately, I chose fear and believed he had taken advantage of me, but I really wanted to believe that he hadn't. I called one more time hoping he would answer, and someone did. It was his roommate, the one who answered the door that first day. It had been over a year, and I had no idea they still lived together. Before I began to speak, the roommate asked, "Who is this?" I replied with my name, and he said, "I'm really sorry to tell you this, but your boyfriend died a couple days ago in a car accident." I was still processing the words when he said he had other people to inform and hung up.

I was in shock and didn't know what to do with what I just heard. I called back, fighting back the tears, and after several rings, he finally answered. He seemed to be upset, and I apologized, but I wanted to know if there was going to be a funeral and if there was a point of contact to send flowers. He said nothing had been arranged and that his family had disowned him years ago, so he had no one. I asked what I could do to help, and he said, "You can't do anything *now*, he's dead."

I kept asking questions about the family and what I could do to help, and he finally said, "You need to stop because I'm getting upset, and this is a lot of responsibility." I apologized again and again, but I needed to know how it happened. He said he was heading west on I-10 and lost control of his car. By the time the paramedics arrived, he had bled to death because a pen had been driven into his heart from the impact. He said it looked like he had been trying to write out a check or something because the checkbook was still in his hand.

I hung up the phone and put my head in my hands, whispering, "No, no," and then began to sob uncontrollably. My selfishness and greed killed him! I was so ashamed of myself. I called my mother in tears sobbing through what must have sounded like the most absurd story! I told her that I loved him and never said it. That he needed my help and I doubted him and left horrible voice messages on his mobile phone. I said he must not have been able to pay his bill, or he would have contacted me. I said he was coming to pay me, and because of my greed and selfishness, he was dead. I'm not even sure my words made any sense to her.

She calmed me down and said to give it a day and then call back to find out if there was a memorial service. She told me there was nothing I could do and that it was God's will. I hung up and sunk into a horrible place. I had killed this young man because I didn't trust him and because I was greedy. I was a horrible person, selfish, and unworthy of love. I was spinning out of control on the floor of my kitchen when the phone rang. It was the roommate calling me back. I picked up sobbingly and said hello.

"Todd?"

I knew that voice.

I'd never heard a dead man speak before. I was traumatized and couldn't make sense of it all. I begged to see him. "No." He said. I begged some more stating I just wanted to hug him. He refused again. "Please let me see you." I said again. He reluctantly agreed and I drove to his apartment. I rationalized that he didn't want to see me because he was afraid or even embarrassed after what he just took part in. That would make sense looking back on all this now but the most bizarre thing to me was that I had just talked to a dead man and I needed to see him breath for myself to believe that he was really alive. I didn't recognize the location of his apartment; in fact I was surprised that I even drove there in the state I was in.

I walked in, he just sat there on the bed in silence. I couldn't believe he was sitting right there in front of me. I wanted to grab and hold him, but he looked as though he didn't want me to touch him, and I can't believe I'm actually writing this, but all I wanted to do was make love to him. We talked for a bit, and I asked to stay, but he said I should leave. I pleaded with him to let me stay. I just wanted to hold him. He wouldn't agree. He said something to the effect that, "Well now you've seen me." I was hurt and confused and a whole bunch of other things. He wouldn't acknowledge my relief or comfort me. I began to feel like I was going to throw up, so, I left.

I was in shock. I sat in the parking lot of his apartment complex with my car running, thinking how pathetic I was to be there and to tell him that I wanted him. What did I do to make him do such a thing? I remember asking God to give me someone just like me a few months before I met him. Looking back, I think I got just what I asked for. He too was manipulative, selfish, desperate, and capable of anything at the expense of others. This was exactly how I felt about myself for coming out and I deserved to struggle. I believed we deserved each other, not in a negative way, but because I believed he could love me as much as I was capable of loving him.

It was 2006, and I was making more money than I had ever before. I had survived coming out, the infection, losing my job, and nearly my family. I was actually beginning to thrive and wanted him to be a part of that. I was willing to accept him for who he was if he were willing to do the same for me. Although I drove away, the damage was done in the form of a traumatic bond that would difficult to break. Before you cast a stone, consider our similarities and the fact that I just spoke to a dead man. He knew this game, and even if he wanted to believe I genuinely loved him, what guarantee did he have that I was any different from every other man who put conditions on their love for him?

I imagined two imperfect people

I decided a relationship was not what I wanted. Besides, the idea that I could simply drop a gay man into my life and continue to live just as I did before coming out was delusional. I had no idea what I was getting myself into or what I was asking these men to do. Most gay men were not ready or equipped to handle what I was bringing to the table. They were wonderful, and I loved them as much as I was capable of, but they didn't stand a chance with me.

I was basically a thirty-five-year-old gay baby. I was still hiding my fear and shame, which made me difficult to deal with, I had unrealistic expectations of myself and them, and I wanted to experience being gay, and that meant more of a single person's life. It was difficult enough for me to live this new lifestyle one weekend and then be a father the next. I could never seem to get it right, and so I frustrated my lovers and ultimately sabotaged relationships because I couldn't do it all or have it all.

For the next two years, I dived right into the gay scene. I had a group of friends who worked hard and played hard. Every weekend, there was a house party, pool party, or circuit party. In fact, we were always partying, filling our bodies full of stimulants to lower inhibitions and enhance every experience. We sought whatever we desired and didn't apologize for it. Hookup apps were becoming more popular, and it was easy to find someone who was looking for the same thing you were.

I began to go to circuit parties where I would be awake for three days in a different city with hundreds of other half-naked gay men. Larger cities had amazing clubs that stimulated your every sensation with environments that supported sexual experiences without identity or accountability. Bathhouses, adult bookstores, and sex parties were all available, and soon I didn't want the man, the house and the "gay family" anymore.

I was burning the candle at both ends and didn't seem to mind. I connected with him a few times during this period. It seemed like he was enjoying the life as well. We didn't operate in the same circles, but circles overlap. It had been almost two years since his resurrection. I'm not even sure how I ended up in his bed; I just remember waking up around two in the afternoon. It was awkward playing catch up again after going so long without seeing him. I told myself I could find whomever I wanted and that he was just another guy, but he wasn't, and I didn't want him to be.

We talked a bit, but I can't remember what about, only that he was seeing someone, and of course, there was some issue that made it okay that we slept together, but that I really should get going. His stories never added up, but I didn't care. Really, I didn't care. I saw myself in him. I wanted to love him and by doing so, love myself. I imagined two imperfect people who would not judge nor hurt each other. I kissed him goodbye and left.

I dont't blame you

It was almost a year later when he called, I had seen him out a few times, but we didn't connect, so I was eager to talk to him. I answered, and we began with basic conversation, and then he got quiet. I asked him what was wrong, and he brought up the last time we saw each other. I figured something had gone wrong with the relationship and it had to do with me being there. That would make sense with him because it being my fault would create an opportunity for him to ask me for whatever he needed at the time. He told me his ex did find out I was there, but that wasn't the reason for the call.

"Well, what is it?" I asked. He explained that he hadn't been feeling well and couldn't seem to shake what he thought was a cold so he went to the doctor. He paused for a moment and then said, "I'm HIV positive." It was difficult to hear him say that. I knew the feelings that went along with those words, and the fact that they were coming from him only amplified what I was feeling.

He went on to explain how it affected his relationship, job, and school and that it had all been very hard to deal with. I told him I was sorry this happened to him and began asking questions to fill the awkward silences. The conversation seemed strained as we both ran out of things to say. Finally I asked him when he found out. He didn't say a date, he just referenced back to the last night I had stayed over. Suddenly, the whole thing felt even worse and then he said it: "I must have gotten it from you."

Those words felt so heavy in the silence that followed. It was even worse that he believed I had given it to him. My heart ached as I thought about all the times that we had sex over the years, and he had never contracted it. At least, I didn't know if he had. I realized we never discussed his status. As far as I knew, the science and discipline had worked. I can count on one hand the number of times I've taken a dose late but never missed it and have remained undetectable since the second month after getting infected.

I asked if he had considered other partners or had asked them. He said he had and that everything lined up with our last sexual encounter. My brain scrambled for more questions, other possibilities and a different outcome but nothing gave me peace. Finally, he said, "I don't blame you, I just wanted you to know." I let that sit with me for a moment and when I realize that didn't feel good either I said, "I have to go." And hung up.I sank into depression, and I never spoke of it again to anyone. I was ashamed, and the only way I knew how to deal with shame was to punish myself, and so I did. I began by sabotaging my relationships because they provided happiness I didn't deserve. I was unworthy of love and naturally questioned their love for me. I'd tell myself that it wasn't going to last for a number of reasons, and since they were eventually going to cheat on me and hurt me (projecting), I may as well beat them to the punch. I had engaged in sex outside of my relationships before, but something had changed. It wasn't about desire, comfort, or pleasure anymore. It was about rejection, grief, and pain.

Get exactly what I deserved

As a child, I was molested, tortured, and raped. I had no power or control over it and had never resolved it. Through a series of sexual experiences, I was introduced to dominant and submissive scenarios. I was uncomfortable in the beginning with some of the things that were done to me. For obvious reasons, I don't like to be scolded, slapped, spanked, or be pinched anywhere, but to feed my disdain, I allowed all of it because I was *choosing* to engage in the activity. The problem was, it wasn't about sexual exploration as an adult. It was about *me* as an adult wanting control of my sexual abuses as a child.

I experimented with different scenarios and partners to find the gratification I was looking for. I was running into a problem: nothing seemed harmful enough to satisfy my self-loathing. I know now it had little to do with self-gratification and more to do with self-destruction

With each experience, I would get bolder and feel more empowered, but I was still holding back. I could see what I wanted to do, but I couldn't surrender to it. My ego was getting in the way. I couldn't allow myself to fully submit to anyone, yet something was pushing me to do so. I tried to see myself as a victim, but for me, that required weakness, and I just couldn't go there. Try as I might, I would continually stop short of what I really needed and deserved for what I was and for what I had done.

It was through the illusion of control that I found a way to trick my ego. The irony of submission is that the control resides in the surrender. As an adult, I could choose to surrender, finding it even more erotic to take someone who appeared to have no sense of power and give it to them in the form of my body. I told myself I would have loved that gift, to have someone entice me into a sexual experience that demanded my dominance. They would construct the situation, orchestrate the experience, command the narrative, and even dictate the outcome. A contrived fantasy with all the elements needed to feel victimized, controlled, and used, when in fact, I was the perpetrator. There was added pleasure in their satisfaction and boosted self-esteem. These were complex emotions that needed dark places to hide and be expressed. I found them and lots of other things in these hiding places. When you seek pain, it finds you, and so will others in pain.

Soon, I met people eager to help me feel different about it all. With my inhibitions, self-respect, and shame suspended, I could get exactly what I deserved. I had temporarily replaced the hate for myself with the illusion of control, putting me in unhealthy sexual and psychological scenarios that allowed me to be molested, abused, and raped over and over again, all the while telling myself that I was in control because I said who, when, where, and how.

I bent all the rules, and by the grace of God, did not break. The tattoo on the back of my neck reads, "Unbreakable" to remind me of the resilience and grace that kept me climbing back out of each hole I had dug. It's extremely difficult to explain why I would choose to do what I did in the first place, to keep digging when I knew I had to climb out every other weekend to be a father. I was playing a dangerous game that most lose. My personal loathing was powerful and could not be denied, yet I promised I would not abandon my children again. I could self-abuse, self-sabotage, and self-defeat as long as I didn't self-destruct.

I learned how to function this way a long time ago. When it was done, I would go down the hallway to the bathroom, shut the door, and lock it. I'd gently place a cool, wet washcloth on the hand-shaped welts. They were bright red against my pale Irish skin, and I could feel the heat radiate through the washcloth just seconds after laying it on my body. I would stay in there as long as I needed, as long as I wanted. It was my rules, my body and my choice.

Stop surviving and
start thriving

I had often thought of doing something more creative for a living. It was going to either be an interior designer, a chef, or a hairstylist. I decided that the world already had Nate Berkus to help them choose throw pillows for their couch and Emeril Lagasse to add a little spice to their meals, so I would become a hairstylist. My former mother in law was a hairstylist and it was always nice to see how amazing people felt after she finished making them feel beautiful. It also resonated with me because a soldier once explained to me why he took such meticulous care of his uniform and appearance. He said that when he looked good, he felt good and that seemed to inspire others around him to feel the same way.

Within a year, I was rid of my business, my house, and most of my friends. I moved into an apartment in Scottsdale just ten minutes from a beauty school and began my new career. I was back on track and determined as ever. There's something about rising from the ashes that motivates me. I believed I was in control of every aspect of my life, but actuality, I was just testing myself to see if I was, in deed, unbreakable.

I spoke to my mother a lot during this time. I'm pretty certain she knew I was scared. I had started over again and that meant I had "stopped" doing something unhealthy or destructive. First, I left the army, then my father's company, and now I was shutting down my insurance agency. It seemed to make perfect sense to her, so she supported me. She didn't need to know the behavior that went along with it. After all, she was my mother and had seen me crash and nearly burn the previous times. All she cared about was that I was happy. I told her not to worry because I was a survivor. I remember her voice on the phone that particular day. It was very stern as she said, "Sweetheart, you need to stop surviving and start thriving." I took it to heart and did just that.

I excelled at doing hair and naturally pushed myself to the limits of my skill and everyone's patience, including the guy I was seeing. Try as I might to enjoy the success, I needed the balance of failure, and that came in the form of another sabotaged relationship. This particular one set the stage for the next. I was made painfully aware of my behavior, and for the first time, took responsibility for my actions.

Marc could have just left without sharing his feelings, and I could have denied him the opportunity to express himself, but I believe he genuinely wanted me to be happy, and although I could not be that person for him, he wanted me to be a better one for myself.

It was a difficult blessing that came at a terrible price, and I remain grateful for his honesty and courage in holding me accountable for my actions. I didn't want to be a wolf in sheep's clothing. I just wanted to be happy, and that needed to start with me. I wasn't used to examining the truth about things. It was always about what I felt, not the facts about where those feelings came from. Knowing what I know now about my past, I can forgive myself for not digging too deeply.

I struggled with the truth about that experience, but it was the truth and not some convenient version of it. My new career kept me focused and was turning out to be so much more than what I had expected. I had entered a competition for six new hairstylists to travel the country in groups of two, sharing their personal stories to inspire others and spread the love for the beauty industry. I won and set off on a new adventure for six months.

I was forty-four years old, paired with a twenty-year-old, bouncing around the country and posting on social media. We spoke to students and stylist of all ages and backgrounds, holding fundraisers and supporting local charities around the country. The mission demanded everything I had because the people we were inspiring deserved it. In their eyes, we were living a dream, and they looked to us for motivation and inspiration. We didn't fail to deliver.

I can't ever remember a time when I shared so much of myself with so many and expected nothing in return. I was doing beautiful work in so many different ways. Not every woman ends up in a magazine or television commercial. In fact, hardly any of them do, but they can be made to feel like that. This was a different kind of giving. It was selfless and genuine, and I was exceptional at it.

Meeting so many young people in the industry made me feel disadvantaged because of my age until my life and business experience became obvious to everyone. Soon, I was sharing with them that life was all about people and the relationships we have with them and how their work could transform lives. I believed it because it was transforming mine. I had life experience and good communication skills that helped me connect with clients. I was a natural.

The work was gratifying, creative, authentic, and in service to others. I could work autonomously, which eliminated competition and minimized doubt. I felt more comfortable sharing with my clients because of the one-on-one time I had with them. I believed I was creating safety in isolation behind my chair when, in fact, I was learning to trust myself and other people.

I could make mistakes and forgive myself without focusing on what others thought or giving energy to how they felt about me. It was just my client and me once a month creating, sharing, and growing. Something magical was happening. I was forming healthy relationships and becoming comfortable in them.

We sat down on that word

I had been on tour for three months and received a call from a Phoenix number I didn't recognize. It was as if I knew who it was, I felt anxious almost immediately as my body began to respond to the thought of him. I really didn't want to pick up, but I kind of had to, right? I toyed with the idea of just letting it go to voicemail, but that felt even worse. I was doing so well and felt like I was in a better place emotionally. I was even seeing someone, and that was going well, too. Nope, avoiding would only prolong whatever was coming, and the best defense was a good offense. The internal dialog went on in my head as the phone continued to ring. Wait, it might not even be him. It could be a client or a referral! For God sake pick up the phone! Who was I kidding? I closed my eyes, took a deep breath and picked up without saying a word. My heart sank when I heard that familiar voice say, "Todd?"

We made some small talk and shared a little about what each of us had been doing. To my surprise, he didn't seem to be attacking me or working some kind of angle, but I still listened closely to everything he said and how he said it. I had grown, after all. I had punished myself, wiped the slate clean, and was becoming the man I wanted to be, a man who thrived.

He mentioned he had been following my recent adventures on social media and that he was proud of me. That was unexpected and nice to hear. I took the opportunity to share all the positive things about it, explaining how I had found my passion, doing great work, and how excited I was about my future. I made it a point to let him know I was happy and creating something new for myself because I was afraid he would make me feel guilty, and I couldn't predict where that would lead emotionally. I figured if I stated that I was in a really good place, he'd think twice about tearing me down or asking me for something I didn't want to give him. Maybe he would feel compassion and abort his mission altogether. Mission? How was it acceptable even to entertain having this man in my life, knowing I could not trust him? I'm sure you're beginning to answer these questions.

When I was finished bringing him up to speed, he asked if I wanted to meet for coffee when I got back in town. There was a long pause as I contemplated seeing him. I have to be honest; I knew what he felt like, tasted like, and smelled like. I told him that I didn't think it was a good idea. I was seeing someone and being on the road so much meant that time together was important, and what little I had, I wanted to spend with him.

He went on to explain that he had some major things happening in his life, and he thought that given all we had shared in the past that it would be nice to catch up without all the drama. I held the thought as I imagined what that would be like together with the truth. Perhaps we both had grown, and he really was the one. Wait, how did I go from, "I'm seeing someone" to "he really was the one?" I went as far as to think that him getting infected was part of God's plan. I held on tight to the hope that it wasn't me and that perhaps he acknowledged that as well. Had we both grown? Had it not been the right time? On and on, I went in my head as a myriad of feelings consumed my body. How did he do this to me?

He broke the silence by acknowledging it might not be the best time to get together but didn't end the call. He had conceded. Or had he? The military term for this tactical maneuver is "faint." Neither of us seemed to want to upset the other by denying a request, so we sat stalemate in our defenses. Someone needed to go on the offense to bring this call and relationship to an end.

In the faint, you deliberately give a little ground, letting the enemy perceive vulnerability so they feel confident enough to commit their forces to the spot you've chosen for engagement. Once they gain a little ground, you relax your defense even more, and with a false sense of security, they rush into your trap. Once in, you slam the door behind them, cutting them off from family, friends, and all other support. Isolated and confused, you now have your enemy right where you want him; all you have left to do is destroy him.

The silence was long and uncomfortable. I don't do well with silence. It requires a lot of discipline and patience to maintain. *Great*, I thought, *I'm already at a disadvantage, and now I need to keep my mouth shut and be patient too?* I was beginning to feel guilty for not being compassionate and wondered if not seeing him was indicative of being weak and not confident in who I was becoming. I tapped my finger one through five repeatedly so I would not be tempted to talk.

He was dangerous to me but then again, all men were. That's what I knew. That's what I was comfortable with. What if I chose to commit? What if I knew what I was getting myself into, and by doing so, could show him that I was willing to go that far for his love? It's what I would want, someone to show me how much they loved me and wanted me. Surely, he would see that I had grown and changed and chose to love rather than destroy myself. Again, I go from him being dangerous to me being enough for him to love.

The Starbucks he suggested wasn't very busy, but then again, it was in the middle of the day. I saw him right away as I walked in. There could have been a hundred people crammed in that coffee shop, and I would have only seen him. He would not acknowledge that if you asked him, he never believed that I actually felt that way about him. My heart was pounding, and it was as if I was seeing him for the first time.

He looked different. He was thinner in a butterscotch and navy, checkered, long-sleeved shirt. The sleeves were folded and pushed halfway up his forearms, and he had decided to leave the second button undone on his shirt, exposing his chest. He always smiled so big, and his teeth were pearl white next to his skin.

As I got closer, I noticed his color was off, and his hair was short, matted, and textured, which was uncharacteristic for a Filipino. Something was wrong, and I immediately assumed the worst as I hugged him. *No, no*, I thought as I held him. We released, and I went right for the obvious, "Are you okay?" I asked.

He softened his smile and said with a deeper voice, "I have cancer." We sat down on that word, and I remained quiet as he went on to explain what he had been going through. The lumps, the fear, and the unknown—it was hard to hear from such a beautiful young man. He described the diagnosis and the timeline of it all. He had finished chemotherapy, and it appeared to go well. He was almost done with radiation, and then he would be tested to see if there were any more tumors in his body.

He went on to explain that he was doing okay and that he had learned and grown a lot from the experience, like most people who get cancer. I just sat and listened, noticing the sickness in his skin, eyes, hair, and even words. He smiled through it all as he continued to explain that it was actually common for men his age to get, especially with the increased risk associated with the introduction of anti-retroviral drugs to treat his HIV. My head dropped along with my heart.

"Hey," he said and continued, "It taught me one more thing." I looked up at him, and he said, "I've loved you since the day I met you, and I think you feel the same way, so if this is my only chance to tell you, then at least I got to say it."

I just looked at him, confused. I think I was confused. So many things were running through my mind. I thought I knew who he was, yet I wanted him to be something different, something better. Did I hear him right? Did he just say he felt exactly the same way I did when we first met? Wait a minute. *Now* you love me after my greed drove you to fake your own death and then pushed you away to deal with HIV and cancer alone? *This is bizarre*, I thought, and yet I found myself entertaining the idea again that God had orchestrated this whole thing to bring us together. Were we made for each other, or did we just deserve each other?

All of this raced through my mind in a matter of seconds, but the silence felt like a lifetime, "Wow, that's a whole lot to process at once," I said.

He said something to the effect of, "I know, but I thought you deserved to hear it." I reminded him that I was seeing someone, and I didn't believe that was going to change with one conversation. We talked for a while more. I held his hand, and I didn't want to let go. He had been struggling, and I felt it. I could also see it on his fingers. When nervous he would bite the cuticle and skin around his nails until they would bleed.

It was hard to see him like this. He was scared and rightfully so. He said his relationship recently ended and that it was all he could do to handle work, school, and treatment. He was a lot of things but lazy wasn't one of them. His was a story of abandonment, and that fear influenced his behavior and motivated him to survive. It also drew me to him like moth to a flame. I had a unique additional "daddy issue," I had abandoned my children and had been reaping what I had sown with my own son. Perhaps I saw redemption in him for that as well.

I considered all the ways he made me feel from the beginning and how he made me feel in that very moment. *WTF was happening? Why was I still here?* I thought to myself. There was no way I could go back to all of that. I had started a new life, and I had embraced a new career and opportunity for my own redemption over self-destruction, loneliness, and shame. I wrapped up the conversation as compassionately as I could and left.

I remember leaving feeling conflicted and telling myself that there was no way this was going to change anything. I felt bad for leaving him in need but was afraid of what I would do or agree to if I stayed. He was sick, hurt, afraid, and alone. But he had also shown me exactly who he was five years earlier, and I needed to believe him. Yes, cancer changes people, and he did reach out to me, but no matter what I was feeling in that moment, I needed to let him go.

That's just it, though. How I felt about him always overruled what I thought, and this was no exception. I had looked into his eyes and saw a hurt little boy reaching out to me. Help me, love me, keep me safe—he needed me! I was certain that in some way I had failed him, and even if I had not, he believed I had, and I should have known better. I should have seen what he needed, been more compassionate, patient, and understanding.

He really wasn't bad, like me he had just made poor choices, and yet here he was, professing his love for me, basically forgiving me for creating all of this sickness and pain. I guess the conversation *had* changed everything because over the next couple of months, I ended the relationship I was in, and within six months of that meeting, moved in with him. I was going to love him, protect him, and take care of him like he had never experienced before. Most importantly, I would never leave him.

PART 8

Two wrongs never getting it right

It was rough right from the start, but we were in love or as capable as we could be. Trust was always an issue. I cheated first, of course. Why wouldn't I? Strike first because it was coming my way soon enough. I had reason to distrust him, and he had reason to distrust me, but that was no reason to do what we did to one another. It was like we tested each other and wanted to see how far we could push the other. The greater the harm caused, the greater the amount of love it took to forgive, and that became an unhealthy dynamic as well.

Things were getting out of hand, and something needed to be done to stop the insanity. I assumed he feared being abandoned, and he assumed I thought he was just with me because he wanted a daddy. Of course, the smartest thing we could do with all this dysfunction would be to get married because that would solve everything, so we did.

He actually asked me to marry him and bought the rings. It was a beautiful gesture, and I felt like he really wanted us to be together. He believed that we could bring out the best in each other and prove to each other and everyone that we were worth it. I believe with all my heart that he wanted that, and I see now that I was incapable of giving it to him. In fact, I had turned the tables on my "daddy" theory and made him step up in ways that were unfair emotionally and financially to balance out what I believed I was giving. I wasn't actually holding up my end of the "bargain" because I was expecting him to meet me equally financially, and he simply couldn't. He tried, but that exacerbated other challenges he was hiding with debt.

He made his mistakes, for sure, but I was going to love him, protect him, and help him become the man I knew him capable of being. Perhaps I should have just loved him where he was at and not tried to "fix" him. But that's what dads do when they don't think of their kids as capable—they fix. I took pleasure in his comfort and security, and I was proud to be there with and for him. He took my name, and that was a powerful gesture to me. I celebrated him in my family, encouraged him, and guided him.

I was so proud of him that I would update my father on his progress in school and business to hear him praise his tenacity and passion. He deserved it. He was a hard worker, and I began to pour myself into his progress. So much so that it began to take energy from my own interests. The more I got involved with his professional success, the less intimate we were. The less intimate we were, the more I needed us to succeed. It was happening again. I was beginning to struggle emotionally so I would push myself harder to compensate, but this time it was twice as damaging because I was pushing him, too.

He had an incredible capacity to love and did show up for me in ways he didn't expect he would have to in the beginning of our marriage. When things were good, they were beautiful, and when they were bad, they were toxic. I assumed the role of loving, protecting, and caring for him, but I was more of a wounded child than either of us could have imagined. How could I love or trust him if I didn't love or trust myself? I questioned everything, just as much as he did. We tested, pushed, and demanded a lot of each other, and actually delivered on our promises for a long time until we simply couldn't anymore.

What played out? Unhealthy sex, compromised integrity, anger, vanity, deceit, drugs, alcohol, sorrow, pain, and the list went on and on. Something else was happening that would have a profound impact on the way our story played out too. I was becoming small.

He was beginning to grow in more ways than one and was no longer the "boy" I met or the young man I married. We had worked hard to build his career, and I had personally coached him and focused a great deal of energy to help him. He tripled his income in just three years and had gained respect and new opportunities that allowed him to travel as I did.

He seemed to be doing well, yet he continued to struggle with self-esteem. When convenient, he would tell me I expected too much from him, competed with him, and that I made him feel less than. That really upset me because all I did was speak praise into him. I know how direct and focused I am, but I didn't want to believe I would ever make him feel less than. But then again, I too was a hurt little boy, so perhaps I lashed out and did make him feel that way. I also made it a point to build him up and even tear myself down to make him feel bigger. It was better for both of us if he felt good. If not, he would withdraw and withhold everything from words to affection. The more he held back, the more desperate I became. There's nothing sexy about being desperate, and to emasculate me was to shame me.

To make matters worse, he began to tell me I didn't desire him anymore and that I was attracted to younger, thinner guys. I would naturally respond with how much I loved and desired him. I would hold his face gently in my hands and say it was him that I wanted and that it had been him from the moment I saw him. I meant it, despite how dysfunctional we had become.

I was beginning to have trouble performing sexually with all of the games and lies. The pressure to perform was awful enough, but then add some passive-aggressive dialog and disappointed body language, and I was crippled emotionally. Actually, I was triggered and felt naked and incapable. I was full of shame, and every time I failed with him, that experience was linked to one in my past. What if he was right, and I wasn't attracted to him anymore? I didn't like to entertain that thought. He was my husband, and I would find a way to make us work.

For most of my life, I felt like I really couldn't be hurt. Of course, that was unrealistic, but I had developed enough defense and coping mechanisms to support that claim. I had always believed I was the strongest person in my relationships—seasoned, resourceful, and capable of weathering any storm—but something was different this time. I had never been so dependent on someone for my happiness or redemption, so when it was suggested that we invite others into our bed, I figured it was better for us to acknowledge what was happening rather than continue pretending.

A compromise was better than a failure, and despite every red flag, we remained together. We were two wrongs never getting it right. He would tell me that I was going to leave him and that I should leave him. To support his words, he would push me away, and yet I would not go, despite all the difficulty, I promised I would not abandon him. I stayed, but to cope, I added my old self- destructive behavior to the collective mess that was our marriage. Soon, he joined me. It seemed we were as much alike as I had always imagined. No, there would be no leaving. Everyone had left us, and I had left my family. It had to stop somewhere. So we would stay and suffer in our dysfunction; it's what we knew how to do.

My daddy issues

I thought of my children and what I had put them through. The more difficulty I had with my husband, the more obvious my failings were as a father. I wanted to make my children strong and resilient. I certainly didn't want to create more victims for the world to chew up and spit out. Since I didn't have the courage to be that for my children, I overcompensated with my husband.

I resisted the urge to give them things in lieu of me because I thought that would make them weak. I also held back a lot when I should have asserted myself as a father. There were moments when a lesson needed to be taught, and I would override my fear and weigh in as a father should but not as often as I should have. I'd also receive the normal level of resistance from them as children and teenagers, but the more they resisted, the more I felt my position had been compromised by my choice to leave. I was afraid they would lash out and say things I wasn't strong enough to hear. It happened frequently in my marriage, and it didn't feel good.

I was also mindful of the way I conducted myself as their father. I didn't want them to feel uncomfortable at school or in public with me. I overreacted in a masculine way as often as I could because I didn't want us to stick out as a gay dad and his uncomfortable kids. How does a gay dad act, anyway? How does a "daddy" act? Was I supposed to sit at the table with the other old men, eat, and check my watch while my "boy" danced and laughed with guys more his age?

I did what I knew how to do, and that was to be strong, have a sense of humor, and get them excited about things like my father did with me. When I was really uncomfortable, I would ask their mother for advice. Jennifer helped a great deal by sharing the concerns and questions they had about me. She never violated their trust but gently guided me to decisions that made the most sense for us all. I would speak with Jennifer often about my marriage. She would kindly remind me how difficult I could be and that a woman loves differently than a man and that her ego didn't need to be fed, only her heart.

I was happy to help and coach him on a number of things associated with finances, education, and his job but being the overachiever that I am, I would go too far, and he would get upset with me. He said I made him feel stupid and less than and again, that would upset me. It was never my intention to make anyone feel less capable, but the way in which I approached challenges was often misunderstood. He learned that this was a weakness and that he could easily make me feel arrogant and attack me for making him feel bad about himself. It had been done to me as a child, and I didn't realize how powerful the shame was in shaming another.

Looking back, I see a lot of themes in the relationships with my children and my husband. I've also done a lot of work identifying my "daddy issues" that oddly enough are driven by my choices and challenges as a father. My husband and I were both emotionally immature and harbored resentment from our past that complicated our differences in age and experience.

I was aggressive, and he was passive aggressive. I was intimidating, and he was manipulative. He would want me to play my role as "daddy" around the other "boys" in his circle of friends and at home when it was convenient, but when he felt insecure or felt inadequate, he needed me to be small, and he knew exactly how to make me feel that way.

He wasn't the only one who could influence feelings. I would go too far, according to some people, but there was no such thing for me, only completion of the task or achievement of the goal. I'm a doer and always have been. It's who I am, and most find it attractive in the beginning. They love the energy, confidence, and drive until they get tired, run out of energy or lose interest. I simply remain focused and committed to the original goal, continuing on without you if necessary. This often makes people uncomfortable. They believe I'm pressuring them or trying to out-do them.

For the record, and with all you've learned about me, it's not my intent to make you feel this way. In fact, at a very basic level, I don't care if you fail. I would not make you feel bad or "less than" about it, I know what that is like. I just want to give you my support and ability because that's one way I show love. If you lose interest and drop off the task, I don't think any less of you. I'm driven to accomplish whatever I start because it's important to that little boy who was degraded for not getting it done.

As a child, I never seemed to get it right. I was ridiculed, punished, and shamed for never being enough, so all I do is try to be more, and if you benefit from it, then that's even better. I realize that all of this appears to be a whole bunch of other things, and it may very well be, but it comes from a place of love. If it makes you feel uncomfortable, then I'll do my best to be mindful of it. I have lived my life feeling less than, believing that I am not enough, and therefore I extend the same gift to you that I've always asked for in return: to love you just as you are. God has given me many gifts and talents, and my heart leaps and sings when I use them.

Miracle

I'm a child sitting on a bench, fidgeting, legs dangling, imagining I'm someone, somewhere, doing something magical. Soon, I'm off the bench and in the dirt with a stick or a rock mixing a potion or designing a battle plan. I don't remember ever wanting to be picked for teams or needing lots of things because I was enough, and I had enough until I was taught something different. God will never give us more than we can handle, but in this life of free will, choices were made and things were done to hurt me. The experiences pushed me beyond what I was humanly capable of handling, and so with grace, the rape was pulled behind the veil of consciousness, freeing a twelve-year-old boy to continue his life for a greater purpose.

That's how God created me: imaginative, fearless, and more than enough. Someone who makes things happen and gets things done. With each life experience, I became more valuable and capable to His divine plan, even if I hadn't accepted a role in it. I look back on all the times I lived in my head as a child, teen, and young adult, and even now, engaging in conversations with myself. I wasn't talking to myself at all; I was talking to Him, and that meant He had always been with me.

I began to "wake up" a year earlier when I stumbled on Sirius XM Channel 128, Joel Osteen. I normally don't listen to anything in the car, but the radio sometimes just comes on when you start it. Lucky me! The message was "Put Action Behind Your Faith," and I realized that I had the right idea all along. I was putting in the work, making things happen, believing in myself, and empowering others, but I was missing one critical element—faith. Not only did I not have faith to carry me through times when I lacked trust, I didn't even have trust! I liked the way Joel delivered his empowering messages. I didn't feel like I had to be driven to my knees to serve, I felt like I could stand and deliver; in fact. I could be a warrior if I wanted to. I downloaded as many messages as I could find and began to play them every morning at the gym strengthening my mind, body, and spirit.

I began to see things in me and in my relationship that I had not seen before, mainly because I was beginning to look at both of us with compassionate eyes. I was tapping into my spirituality void of guilt, blame and shame. It was an entirely different experience and way of thinking for me. The biggest connection for me was that a father wants the best for his children, and He loved me as I loved my children. Something was changing in me and although I had spent forty years running away from home, suddenly all I wanted to do was be there. With each step toward Him, I let go of the people and things that no longer served me to focused on my marriage.

I introduced what I was learning to my husband and related it to our relationship. I realized we had no campus, no covenant, and no safe place to be together. Our home was simply a place to avoid each other and sleep until work took us away again. I was incredibly indecisive when it came to doing anything. I couldn't pick a place to eat, movie to see or topic to discuss because I was afraid of getting it wrong. I had become so small, I had become someone he wouldn't want to love but that was going to change now that I had a little faith.

Faith gave me hope and I began to see that things could be different, better, and even though my faith was small, I believed that if I put enough action behind it, our marriage could be saved. I believed for a miracle to end the pain, heal the wounds, and give me back the man of my dreams. I believed with everything I am that my blessing was coming; I just didn't know it would come the way it did.

They had met six weeks earlier. I was actually there when they met and remembered thinking to myself that he was just my husband's type. I hadn't even finished the thought in my head when a client of mine introduced him as his husband. When the truth came out, everyone knew about the affair but me. Despite visiting me twice for a haircut and color, my client said nothing about their romance because he was apparently threatened by his husband to be cut off from his credit cards and have his BMW taken away. *Wow*, I thought. *Control, threats, and perks. Now that's a daddy.*

With me, he was building up his body, extending his travel, and beginning to express concerns about his self-esteem and identity. I was concerned, especially when he would make it sound like I was the source of his anxiety. The truth is that I *was* the source of his anxiety, and he had already decided to leave. I'm assuming the little boy in him couldn't just leave; he had to make sure the blame was at least evenly placed between us so that he could live with his choice. In all fairness, he had gotten all he could get out of me. I had plateaued on many levels because of the guilt, and shame associated with our entire relationship. I had determined that I didn't deserve anything or anyone better and really had nothing left to give him. Still, I was hoping for a miracle.

It wasn't so much that it happened; it was the deception and hurtful way it was done. He informed me on my fiftieth birthday that he had met someone, and they were just friends. He had decided that he needed space to figure out what he was feeling and to understand better what was making him so unhappy. He said he didn't feel sexy or good about himself. I told him I thought he was beautiful and sexy, and we could figure this out together. He said he would move his things out of the apartment over the weekend after dropping me off at the airport. I was heading to Las Vegas the next day for training, and it all seemed to work out perfectly for him.

I expressed my desire to work it out again, but he was insistent on separating, at least for the summer he said. I reminded him of a rule we established a while back. He made it a habit of leaving our bed and sleeping on the couch when he was angry with me. I said that if we were not worth figuring out a problem before going to bed together, then there wasn't much point of being together. Besides, it was unbearable torture to be left alone and ignored, and he knew that hurt me.

I thought hard on what I was about to say, but I knew it needed to be said. I told him that there would be no separation, and if he wanted to leave, it meant a divorce. He asked me if I was sure about that, and at that moment, I realized he had gotten *me* to end it with that ultimatum. He paused as if not expecting it. Then he smiled halfheartedly and said, "If that's what you want."

The hurt was settling in. I could feel it rising up in my body as I considered that he was already gone. "There's one more thing." I said. The smirk on his face disappeared when he heard me say, "I want my name back." I could tell by his response he hadn't considered that as a possibility as if I were a bag, watch or plane ticket acquired along the way. I visualized him introducing himself in a bar somewhere with *my* name, and I drove the point home by adding, "It's my name, my father's name, and my children's name, and if you're not my husband, you're not a Kane."

He got up from the table and walked into the bathroom. I followed him. He turned on the shower, took off his clothes, and began to clean his face in the mirror. He had been working out, and his body was perfectly groomed. I asked him what I could do to make him want to stay. He said I couldn't do anything; it was about him, and he just didn't know what was wrong. He said he didn't like what he saw when he looked in the mirror while he leaned naked over the sink, back arched as he meticulously plucked one of his eyebrows.

I grabbed him, pulled him away from the sink, and pressed him against the wall with my body. I paused, I wasn't sure of myself, but I didn't want to lose him. He didn't resist, so I pressed my body fully into his, and we began to kiss. His hands moved to my neck and mine to his lower back, and away we went just like it used to be. He took my kiss and gave as much back, if not more, as our bodies began to move together. I felt him get aroused against my leg, his breath quicken, and his grip tighten on my neck. I opened my eyes, broke the kiss, and with heavy breath said, "Seems like you're doing just fine now."

Instantly, his expression changed as he pushed me away, snapping back into character: the confused, abused, broken, opportunistic little victim, and said, "You don't understand what it's been like for me!" "Then tell me!" I said, getting no response as he hurried to find something to put on his body. I remained in the doorway of the bathroom with water running and steam building as my imagination ran wild. I took a deep breath and asked, "Are you sleeping with him?" I knew the answer, but I wanted to hear him say it. He stormed through the doorway of the bathroom where he left me and said, "Oh, like I can just meet someone and start having a healthy sexual relationship with them, right? No! You took care of that for me a long time ago." And there it was.

He dropped me off at the airport the next day, I knew he was going back to our apartment to get his things and leave because it had been discussed the night before. He didn't even kiss me goodbye; he just gave me a shallow hug, and turned to walk away. I held on for as long as I could, feeling his arm slip through my hand all the way to my fingers. I curled the tips as far around his as I could. This would be good time for that miracle I thought as he slipped away. For a moment, I thought I got it when he stopped at the car and looked back at me but he just smiled and said, "Have a good trip." I swore it was my heart breaking when I heard the car door shut. I felt nauseated as my knees began to give a little. I guess it was better than being drug across a bar floor. I couldn't have loved him more I thought to myself, but I could have loved him better.

Numb

When I returned four days later, I dreaded walking in the apartment. I had no idea what I would find or how I would feel. I opened the door, and nothing seemed to have changed. I went into our bedroom, and only his clothes and shoes were gone. I looked in the spare bedroom, the bathroom and the kitchen but no change there either, and then I looked out the back door and saw a large garbage bag full of his clothes that he just threw away. When I turned and shut the door, I saw the note on the chalkboard that read, "I'm so sorry. I will always love you."

The bed seemed to have arms, and I seldom broke its grip. Memories and feelings were ripping into my conscious and began to consume me. I had no control of my emotions and soon my body would follow suit. My neck was stiff, my left arm was numb, and my legs often swelled so much that it was difficult to bend or sit down. What was happening? I would wake up drenched in sweat and sometimes in tears. I used every tool I had to change my thoughts and feelings, to simply get it together, but I could not. Leaving the apartment helped but, ultimately, I would return and be right back where I left, in pain. I knew what sad, angry, and numb felt like, but this was different. This was hopelessness.

My coping mechanisms were all self-destructive and usually kicked in when I had something to lose. In those situations, I had stored up mental, physical, and emotional resources to tear into, but now I had none. It was also painfully obvious that I was trapped in everything that reminded me of us. He seemed to be everywhere and nowhere at the same time. I walked aimlessly around the house, never completing a task or a thought without getting pulled into a memory that ultimately led to my failure as a husband.

It wasn't long before I started tapping into the past, digging up old wounds and saying them out loud to myself to make sure I felt them completely. I was in the darkness and would often just sob and say, "Please, God, make it stop." How long could I keep this up? I even wrote in my phone on 6/12/2018: "Dear God, I would never just quit, but if you're done with me, I'm ready to come home." I never allowed myself to feel hopeless. I wasn't wired that way, but recognizing it was frightening to me, and so I reminded myself that faith gives you hope and I really needed it now.

Five

I started at nine in the salon that morning and needed to hand out a business card or two before the day got away from me. I play this little game with myself to continually get new clientele by placing five business cards in my pocket each morning with the intent to have them all gone by the end of the day. Those that are left over are rolled over, so it makes sense not to procrastinate, or your pocket will get full pretty quickly. I'd feel them in my pocket and think, *Out with the cards, in with the clients!*

It may seem simple enough to get rid of just five cards a day if you stick them on car windows or neatly fan them out on the counter of a woman's restroom, which I've done. No, I have to give the card to a person during a conversation specifically about their hair. How I get to the hair is the fun part, and I love playing this little game. It makes sense, right? If I'm going to be your hairstylist, I need to convince you to come see me. After all, you are most likely seeing someone else, and it will take some doing to get you to switch to me.

Regardless of the product or service, it's a sale, a transfer of feeling that results in them reaching into their pocket, pulling out a dollar, and giving it to me instead of someone else.

First, I have to approach a stranger, connect with them, point out something about their hair that I would change, and then convince them to let me do it. Oh yeah, let's not forget the importance of picking the right moment to approach.

It's even more exciting to approach two or more women sitting together. Imagine the possibilities and lessons to be learned if you are not successful. It can go sideways quickly, and you need to be fully present and authentic. Any slip could insult a person who is now holding your business card. I would share this with stylists all across the country, and they would say, "Oh my God, I would be terrified to do something like that!"

I'd reply, "If you believe in your abilities and your intention is to help them look and feel their best, you have nothing to fear." And so I play my little game of five cards five days a week. I know, five is a thing with me.

This day would be no exception as I finished my coffee at one of my favorite coffee shops just three minutes from my salon. I wrapped up the other half of my breakfast burrito, and scanned the room for a new client. She was just a few tables away sitting with another woman. Both could benefit from working with me, but the blonde (natural gray), looked approachable, was facing me, and appeared to be in command of the conversation they were having. Yes, she was the one!

I stood up and slid my chair back so that the metal legs would drag against the concrete. The high-pitched sound made everyone with ears and teeth glance in my direction. It worked, and I smiled apologetically as she looked at me and smiled back. I reached into my pocket, surprised to find only one card. Well, I had been off my game a bit with all that had happened. There were two women, and you never want to leave one out, or they may feel rejected. In situations like this, one can say no just to be polite to the other. Also, the blonde was clearly in a position to influence the brunette, so she would most certainly choose her over me in a heartbeat.

One card, two women, and three minutes. "I got this," I said under my breath, and over to their table I went. "Pardon me, ladies. I know you're in the middle of something, but I'm a hairstylist, and I was over there imagining all the beautiful things I could do with your hair," I said, directing the first few words toward the blonde then continuing to speak as I turned to include the brunette.

I paused and let my approach settle in. They smiled politely and then looked at each other with strange faces. *Here it comes*, I thought to myself. It's always the same, and I actually got a kick out of each unique response. "Oh my God, are you saying my hair is awful?" said the blonde as she grabbed the damaged ends of her hair. The brunette lowered her head, pulled on her bangs, and attempted to look at them before letting them drop into her eyes and then blowing them out of the way with a defeated exhale. I smiled, again letting that all set in for a second, and then laughed politely before directing my response to the blonde.

"No, not at all. In fact, I get that a lot when I approach women who are not terribly inspired by their hair," I said and then went on to explain how much healthier her hair would look if she maintained the ends frequently with a disciplined stylist who would help her continue to grow it out. Women are always growing out there hair when they don't have a stylist to inspire them.

Then I moved to the brunette, "And you have beautiful eyes, I would love to reshape those bangs and bring up the overall length to focus on your cheekbones and smile." Then, I put my only card on the table between them both, and said, "I have one left, but I didn't want to miss the opportunity to help both of you look and feel your best." I then recommended one take the card and the other take a picture of it with their phone.

The blonde grabbed her phone first and introduced herself as Valerie. She said she was actually looking for someone new to do her hair. I told her that it must be fate, and then asked if she wanted me to type in my Instagram handle for her to make it easier to find me. She agreed and handed me her phone. "It's just easier this way." I said as I selected the "follow" button and handed it back to her.

"Is this you, ToddKaneHair?" she asked.

"Yes, I'm Todd, and my salon is just around the corner," I explained. I thanked them for their time, wished them a happy day, and headed to work. Success!

Unforgiven

I saw her name on my schedule, but I didn't recall meeting a Valerie recently. I looked at the service selected, but it just said base color, partial highlight, and haircut. Perhaps she was a referral or found me online, either was a good source to get new clients and keep busy. The pain in my shoulder and arm was intensifying. I had made an appointment with the VA to get everything checked, but it would be another week before that happened.

I recognized her immediately when she walked in. She even hugged me and said she had been looking forward to her appointment. We laughed about the day we met almost three weeks earlier. I asked what happened to her friend, the brunette, and she said she was actually her client and that she struggled with making decisions. I smiled and nodded my head acknowledging to myself that my original perception of the two was correct, and then we both began to laugh as if she was reading my mind. It was an instant connection.

I began the consultation from where I left off at the coffee shop. We made a few decisions about what to do this service and what we might do on the next, depending on the results and how she felt about it during the weeks after. I applied her base color and then started to highlight her hair using bleach lightener and foils. We talked a bit during the process, but I was having trouble keeping my arm up, and I was wincing from time to time. I would also get distracted with emotion and thoughts that I did not realize were so obvious to others.

She asked me a couple times if I was all right, and I said yes. It happened enough that I was running out of jokes and excuses. Finally, I finished and set the timer for thirty minutes. Fifteen had already passed and together would ensure the total of forty-five minutes needed to fully process the base color and cover all of her gray hair.

She was new, so I needed to be on my game to hold the space, but I was in all kinds of pain. She asked about the arm, and I told her I must have done something in the gym to irritate it. She mentioned that she had a similar experience and that it was related to her neck, and she actually had surgery. I didn't' want it to be anything she could relate to, so I slipped and told her about the lack of sleep and my legs, and then I just got quiet.

Normally, I would sit behind them, and we would talk into the mirror, but she turned my big red chair around, and with a head full of shiny foils said, "I know we just met, but what's going on?" I was caught off guard. Here was a stranger, a new client, sitting in my chair in what had become my only safe place, my sanctuary, asking me what was going on. I didn't know how to respond. This was my space. I'm in command here. Nobody turns that chair around on me. I was leaning against the counter where I mix all my color, my arms folded, and pain racing through my head, neck, and arm. My legs hurt, and I really didn't have anywhere to go or any way to avoid the question. I smiled politely and said, "I'm good."

"What does 'good' mean?" she said kindly. I glanced out the window, and then shifted my sight to the floor and eventually the door. It was open. I always leave it open so people can see and hear and experience what I do but this wasn't anything I wanted to share. It was awkward standing there with her looking at me. What was I supposed to do, stall for another twenty-eight minutes?

"You don't have to tell me, but I'm here," she said. I made a pass with my eyes around the room again, finishing at the open door. I felt incredibly uncomfortable and exposed. My body was revving up and everything started to hurt more. I was trapped! I was decisively engaged. I couldn't "flight," and I certainly couldn't "fight!" She asked, "How many cards did you have in your pocket that day we met?"

It all came back to me, the realization I only had one card, the sliding of the chair, the bangs, the phone. "Just one," I said.

"And here I am," she replied with a gentle smile. Again avoiding with the eyes and now some deep breaths. I felt so threatened, yet I wanted just to let it all out. I was rocking back and forth from side to side now, arms folded, sweat showing on my shirt at the neck and chest. I told her that my husband left me. That's exactly how I said it. It's how I began nearly every sentence recently. I was a horrible victim and even worse about hiding it. The stress was having its way with my body, and I couldn't control any of it.

I went on to say that it was "all good" now. I had decided he was dead to me and that I had put that part of my life behind me. She didn't seem convinced and suggested that he wasn't dead and that I hadn't put it behind me. In fact, he was alive and well and in total control of my life. I shook my head and looked down at the floor.

She continued, asking me how many times I had been in this spot before? How many times had I had the opportunity to face my fear and chosen to avoid it? I said nothing. She gave it another second to sink in and then said, "What did you do?" It was hard to stand there. I had been overheating since she turned the chair on me. I looked at her again and then the open door. Again she said, "What did you do that you think is so awful that you deserve to live with this pain?"

I was scrambling to escape the situation, but I was stuck. Where did this woman come from, and why was she here? "I can't say," I whispered as I began to rock frantically back and forth on my feet. She reminded me that I had a choice in everything, including the choice to stay in this conversation.

I looked down at the square tile I was standing in and realized I had been here before, many times as a boy and a man. I had felt ashamed and less than most of my life, but to acknowledge it at that moment in front of a stranger made me feel defeated. I finally walked over and shut the door, then returned to my spot. Rocking back and forth from left to right foot, I felt like a child. I was not a crier, and I certainly wasn't going to give this stranger my tears. "I can't say it," I told her in a weakening voice.

"All right, I'm going to make this easy for you," she said. I looked up at her childlike as she asked. "Do you believe in God?" I was surprised that I said yes without hesitation. She said all of this struggle would end if I simply asked Him for forgiveness. I told her that it wasn't that easy, and she said, "Why not?"

"Because you can't just walk into a confessional, spill your guts, say a few Hail Mary's, and be done with it!" I said sternly. By this time, I was starting to pace and became verbal. I asked her WTF was happening right now. "It's not that easy!" I said, to which she quickly replied, "Ask him for forgiveness and assume responsibility for your life." I started to weep. I told her that I had lived my entire live unforgiven in guilt and shame and I didn't know any other way to live!

"If not now, then when, Todd?" she said firmly. I couldn't hold it back anymore. I closed my eyes and tears rolled down my cheeks as I surrendered to the pain pushing these words out of my mouth, "Dear God, please forgive me for abandoning my family, for getting HIV, for him getting it, and the cancer." I said I hated myself and that I wanted that pain to stop. I stood there drenched in sweat and tears. Valerie remained calm as she whispered that everything was going to be all right.

I felt like a child, crying and gasping for breath. I desperately needed to wipe my nose and face, but it didn't really matter. In fact, nothing seemed to matter at that moment. My breathing eventually slowed down, and I wiped off my face. As my body cooled and my heart settled, I realized I had never said those words before. I wanted to feel embarrassed and ashamed, but I didn't. She told me to check my watch and so I did, it was exactly

6:15. She said to write that down so I would never forget this moment. I took one of my business cards and grabbed a pin. I was surprised to write, 6:15 on 6/15. I told her about the date and time and she just smiled. She then asked me how I felt, but I didn't really know. I tried to describe all the different emotions running through my mind and body but couldn't settle on just one amazing thing. I sighed, surrendered and dropped my head. We were both quiet for minute as my body caught up with my spirit. Then she said, "Hey, look at me." I lifted my eyes to see her kind smile as she explained, "That's what forgiveness feels like."

Someone once told me not to share too much with my clients because they were there to have *you* listen to *them*. That's true to an extent, but all of my clients are handpicked, and even if they were new to me, they most likely came referred from a friend. It was divine, all of it: becoming a hairstylist and rediscovering the value in each beautiful human interaction—one card, two women and a divine connection.

Beauty changed my life without me even realizing it. What I do is love, beautiful inside and out. All the times I showed up, held space, and poured my love into them was returned tenfold. My clients were patient, kind, and loving. When I had a rough day, they would check me with a smile, "Now, you said you were going to make me a little darker this time and add some copper, remember?" "Oh, yeah," I'd say, and then they'd point out that I had asked them to remind me. It was sweet to see them take such care of my emotions during that difficult time.

When I'd travel the United States educating hairstylists, I would tell them to be professional and authentic because what you project to the world is what you attract. It was incredibly gratifying to realize I was loved, trusted, and respected by my clients. I connected with them every month and expressed myself emotionally and in creative ways I had never done before. I felt the beauty in my work seeing the way they left feeling about themselves, and how they carried that into their other relationships at home, work, and play. My chair became a sacred space, and when you sat in it, magical things happened.

Truth gives you peace

Coming out did not end the game of hide and seek for me. I didn't find that I was liberated, transformed, or even safe. On the contrary, I was more confused and frightened than ever. I didn't know where to seek men like me other than in bars, and those were not the best places, but I didn't know that.

I had begun hiding at a very young age, and although I came out at thirty-two, I felt like an awkward adolescent again. I lacked experience and the emotional resources of family and friends. I had isolated myself and worked overtime to hide my sexual identity and desires. Learning the extent of abuse by my stepfather was life changing, but it also helped me understand why I made so many self-destructive choices throughout my life. The molestation by the neighbor boy and the rape by my stepfather created an unhealthy association between men and sex. Although it felt natural to be with men, I struggled with intimacy and trust. I wanted to believe I was capable of loving another man, but I had challenges I didn't even know existed.

As a teenager I began creating space and independence in hopes of living my life as a homosexual. With the abuse suppressed, I believed it was possible. I remember actually thinking I could move away to college and live any life I chose. My stepfather had lost his hold on all of us as his marriage to my mother collapsed. We had survived, and I felt empowered by the possibility of living without fear.

I went to church with my mother on Sundays. It was important to her, and we were the last survivors of both marriages still living together. I had rebelled a couple of years earlier when I was supposed to get confirmed in the Catholic Church, but with my stepfather gone, I wanted to be closer to my mom, and so at the age of 17, I did it. It was something my mother wanted, and it made me happy to do it for both of us. She was always strong in her faith, and sharing that experience with her allowed us to move forward together. After all, I wasn't the only person abused in that relationship.

When AIDS engulfed us with fear, it changed everything for millions of people around the world. It was the early 80s, and in an instant, we were afraid to breathe, touch doorknobs, use drinking fountains, and certainly not get anywhere near a homosexual. I simply did not have enough courage or love of myself to overcome all that.

I never revisited that time in my life. I have, on numerous occasions, asked myself the question as to why I chose the path I did. I have punished that young man with my adult expectations, never putting myself back in his shoes, at that age, until now. I was afraid, and I had every right to be. AIDS was a monster, and so was my stepfather. It didn't matter that I couldn't remember specifics, my body and subconscious always reminded me when triggered by associated fears of sickness and pain.

With each revealing chapter of this book, my faith grows. I don't contaminate my present with decades of doubt, nor do I go back and judge my younger self anymore. With each new experience, I help pull that five, seven, twelve, and thirty-two-year-old into the light. I'm patient and kind to them. I love and forgive them. Most importantly, I don't forget them when things get difficult. I connect with all of my fears, acknowledging them, dealing with them, and then make the next best choice for all of us.

Shame and self-loathing are not a part of God's plan. We're not born afraid; we're taught to be afraid. I was preyed upon, and those experiences turned what was for me a natural attraction to men into a shame and fear-filled existence. I have an incredible capacity to love, and now that I've shared that love with myself, I see it possible everywhere in my life.

This new love of myself has also allowed me to accept that the dysfunctional same-sex experiences of my past did not make me gay. They were traumatic experiences that stunted my emotional growth resulting in codependent behavior and unhealthy choices that negatively impacted my life and others. I am not proud of all the things I've done, but with better understanding, I'm not ashamed of them.

Dealing with negative experiences is necessary for growth. If we don't do the work, our stories trap us in an emotional space that robs us of a healthy present. I believe this is why many of us do not fully engage in LGBTQ+ issues that could potentially move us forward as a culture. To do so requires a sense of self that we may not have fully developed yet. It's important and okay to take the time needed to heal but many of us cannot do that on our own. Friends and family are a good place to start but as I've mentioned earlier, these resources may not be available nor have the expertise we need to heal. Counseling will allow you to engage yourself in a productive and objective way. Only then, when we stand comfortably and confidently in our truth as individuals and a community will we realize our true power.

Our stories and the lessons they teach can benefit future generations. Shame lives in silence, and so it is our voices that will keep it at bay with love, integrity, and understanding. We must choose our words carefully, all of us, so we deliberately speak love and inclusivity into our children and each other. By creating safe, healthy, environments we all grow as we learn from each other and encourage authenticity void of harmful labels.

Prejudice and homophobia exist and possibly always will. Therefore, it is in our best interest to have a politically educated and active LGBTQ+ community that votes. Talking is incredibly important and effective if we are mindful of our words and use them to unite rather than divide. It is also critical that we put action behind our words and vote to prevent and eliminate discriminating laws that deny sexual minorities and all minorities' socio-economic advantages available to others. It is through engagement that we remain connected to the healthy and loving sources of family, friends, and each other to share and promote our incredible culture and the diverse gifts and talents we bring to the world.

Choose to acknowledge your fears and articulate your truth in a way that will best serve you. Live authentically and inspire others to do the same. When possible, step in and help those who struggle; don't assume they will just find their way. Teach them to navigate their lives with intention and accept responsibility for their choices. Guide them through challenges and then love them by showing the lesson each provides.

Revelation

I've lived most of my life with secrets. Fear, shame, and guilt have crippled me in so many ways. As a child, I was shaped by the belief systems and fears of others and learned to hide my feelings, keep secrets, and suppress my sexual desires. When that didn't work, I punished myself for being less than what I believed others wanted me to be.

All of those words mattered to us growing up, and they still matter today. Are you hiding because of words you've heard or are afraid to hear? Are you reckless and irresponsible with your language? It's not uncommon, so be mindful of the people around you, especially children and accept responsibility as an adult to actively protect them from ignorance and harm. I invite you to choose your words carefully and simply allow yourself and others to live authentically without objection and interference. Set your intention to acknowledge, process, and overcome your fears to live your truth and not rob another person of theirs.

There's no truth in fear. It is true that we can be afraid. And it is true that there are things in this world that can harm us. It is also true that our primal instinct of fight or flight remains to override our advanced cognitive ability to think ourselves into harm's way. For those fears, we can rely on nature to protect us, and for others associated with potential threats like plane crashes, car accidents or armed conflict, we can prepare and protect ourselves with deliberate choices. For everything else, we can choose to see fear as a complex emotional response that is riddled with un-truths, an acceptable place to hide our inability and unwillingness.

For example, take a moment to thoroughly evaluate something you are afraid of. I'm suggesting getting into the details of who, what, when, where, why and how. If we are honest with ourselves, we can isolate the source of fear and perhaps see it as a choice we are unwilling, unprepared, or unable to make. By mistaking a lack of action for fear, we feel relieved of responsibility for not doing anything and make a case for avoiding or holding on to that fear. It doesn't serve anyone to remain afraid.

I was afraid of how people would perceive me, so I saw myself through the eyes and minds of others, wanting to be loved, accepted, admired, and guided. Unfortunately, when you try to be all things to all people, you end up being nobody to yourself. Your happiness and worth depend on others, and therefore leave you feeling incomplete and dissatisfied.

In addition, where is the accountability and responsibility for your life? What kind of coping skills do you develop? And whom are they ultimately serving? To lose your sense of self is very disturbing to me. I think of all I've accomplished in my life and yet never felt like I was enough. Why? Because I wasn't accomplishing these things for me; I was accomplishing them for others so they would love and accept me. If you don't love and respect yourself, you are limited in your capacity to love and respect others.

Everything in this book played out in one form or another in my last marriage, and in the end, there was no God and no compass to guide us. We wanted marriage equality, but we didn't necessarily want equality in our marriage. We pick and choose the rules we find convenient and ignore the ones that are not. Integrity, respect, and monogamy are not negotiable characteristics relative to age, gender, or sexual orientation. Our marriage didn't fail because of a complicated gay culture or harmful past experiences, it failed because we lied and made choices that did not honor or support our love for each other.

I thought God had given me exactly what I deserved but as always, he had given me just what I needed – the realization that I was living my life in the grip of an accuser. To break free from the lie of not being enough, everything I falsely believed in would have to be removed before the truth was revealed. My accuser was just another frightened, abused little boy. I could not give him what he needed, nor could I fix him on my own. I'm not even sure I ever really loved him. All those years, all those choices and all those lies, I remained with him, hopelessly filling a soul that without faith, was a bottomless cup. Finally, God readied me for the truth and brought me to my knees to face my accuser. To my surprise it wasn't the neighbor boy, my stepfather or my ex-husband, it was me.

Find

God pulled back the veil of lies and revealed the one Truth that holds no fear, shame, or pain, only love. My family did not reject me, my lovers did not deny me, and others did not think less of me for being gay. I did. It was me. It had always been me accepting then rejecting myself in a constant battle with self-worth perpetuated by harmful words and actions of people who should have, or simply didn't, know better.

I isolated, sabotaged and punished myself to feed a pain I didn't know existed. I hid in dark places and sought out terrible things only to find more of the same. As my game of hide & seek became more and more complex, I felt less and less capable of feeling joy and love. Finally, I felt I had no more to give to the charade, and if I was not careful, I would fail and nobody would be able to save me, admittedly not even myself.

I often believed I was one failure away from losing myself all together. I had succumbed to fear and empowered others with the one choice only I could make—loving myself. My faith gives me hope and truth gives me peace. The truth is I have always been enough. I am special, I am a gift, I am Todd Kane and as it turns out, the miracle I was hoping for.

APPENDIX

Resources

Organizations that magnificently support our community and its allies. Connecting with any chapter will help you find resources in your local area or provide assistance wherever and whenever you are in need.

GLAAD

Gay Lesbian Alliance Against Defamation
5455 Wilshire Blvd # 1500
Los Angeles, CA 90036
(323) 933-2240
http://www.glaad.org/
For over 30 years, GLAAD has been at the forefront of cultural change, accelerating acceptance for the LGBTQ community.

https://www.glaad.org/resources
Relevant, trending and various online articles and publications

https://www.glaad.org/resourcelist
Link to LGBTQ list of resources in categories including: Politics, Bisexual, Youth, Military, Transgender, Aging, Legal and General

PFLAG
PFLAG National Office
1828 L Street, NW, Suite 660
Washington, DC 20036
Main Phone: (202) 467-8180
Fax: (202) 467-8194
https://pflag.org/
PFLAG is the first and largest organization for lesbian, gay, bisexual, transgender, and queer (LGBTQ+) people, their parents and families, and allies.

GLSEN
GLSEN, Inc.
110 William Street, 30th Floor,
New York, NY 10038
info@glsen.org
212-727-0135
https://www.glsen.org/
GLSEN works to ensure that LGBTQ students are able to learn and grow in a school environment free from bullying and harassment.

Educator Resources
https://www.glsen.org/resources/educator-resources

Student Resources
https://www.glsen.org/student-and-gsa-resources

Phoenix Chapter
https://www.glsen.org/chapter/phoenix
facebook@glsen.phoenix

PLANNED PARENTHOOD
https://www.plannedparenthood.org/

LGBTQ Services:

https://www.plannedparenthood.org/get-care/our-services/
lgbt-services

PRIDE GUIDE ARIZONA
MC Publishing Inc.
PO Box 45243
Phoenix, AZ 85064
Arizona@ThePrideGuides.com
Phone: 602-466-2501
Toll Free: 888-830-3022

http://gayarizona.com/
The Pride Guides® are corporately based in Arizona where we
first launched, and we publish online and in print versions of our
guides as a resource for the LGBT community and those wishing
to connect with our community.

1N10
1101 N. Central Ave. Ste. 104
Phoenix, AZ 85004
(602) 400-2601
www.OneNTen.org
A source and support organization for the LGBTQ youth and
people of all ages in the Valley of the Sun.

ARIZONA STATE UNIVERSITY LGBTQ COALITION
1290 ASU Memorial Union Building
Room 340
Tempe, AZ 85281
www.Facebook.com
The LGBTQA Coalition at ASU is home to the many lesbian,
gay, bisexual, trans, and queer organizations and their allies that
impact the ASU community.

AUNT RITA'S FOUNDATION
2700 N. 3rd St., Ste. 2012
Phoenix, AZ 85004
(602) 882-8675
www.AuntRitas.org
Helping to support Phoenix area AIDS service organizations.

DEAF QUEER MEN ONLY
11435 W. Buckeye Rd. Ste. 104
Avondale, AZ 85323
623-208-4341
www.DQMO.net

Providing a nurturing space for multicultural Deaf Queer Men to gather, build networks, share emotional support and expand knowledge about civil rights, health, leadership and multi-identities issues.

NATIONAL DOMETIC VIOLENCE HOTLINE
1-800-799-SAFE (7233) 1-800-787-3224 (TTY)
www.NDVH.org
(LGBT) National Hotline
1-888-843-4564
www.GLBTNationalHelpCenter.org

LOS ANGELES LGBTQ CENTER
https://lalgbtcenter.org
Los Angeles, CA

We are an unstoppable force in the fight against bigotry and the struggle to build a better world, a world in which LGBT people can be healthy, equal, and complete members of society.

GAYLESTA
https://gaylesta.org/
San Francisco, CA

The Psychotherapist Association for Gender and Sexual Diversity, was founded in 1987. GAYLESTA has grown to include over 300 mental health professionals and one the oldest and largest collection of individuals focused on LGBTQ mental health. Our membership collectively offers a range of services, experience, specializations, and expertise.

Mom

After a six-month battle with cancer, I arrive at my mother's side after she began morphine injections to eliminate the physical pain associated with her death on June 10, 2014. I struggled with the idea that she didn't appear to hear me but she did. This is what I wrote on the plane ride back to Arizona about the experience.

Four long beats of the clock, a labored breath and a sigh. She's somewhere in between - more there then here now. Three hours, meds, turn, and repeat. Four long beats of the clock, a

215

labored breath, and a sigh. One, two, three, four I'd count in my head, take a breath and then I'd sigh. The suns coming up now and my mind wanders like a child - *how many, how much, how come mommy?* All I can think of are the countless vents of fear and frustration to clear my heart and head she patiently labored thru. Only when it appeared I'd gotten it all out of my system she would ask me, "Are you done?" I'd pause to make sure I didn't miss anything then say, "Yes." She'd say, "It's going to be ok sweetheart, I love you". When I'd storm the grocery cart with Fruit Loops and Lucky Charms she'd say, "You don't need all that sugar honey, you're sweet enough". I'd smile and run them back for Corn Flakes. I heard her say, "Have a happy day!" every morning as I ran out of the house. There are many moments like these spinning around in my head on this early morning in June. I count out six long beats of the clock and listen for a labored breath. I lean in close to feel her exhale and then whisper, "Are you done mommy?" I swear I feel her squeeze my hand and so I say, "It's going to be ok sweetheart, you can go now."

Dad

I was preparing to step into an incredible opportunity as a platform hair stylist in Orlando, Florida at the beginning of 2016. In preparation to serve nearly 2500 hairstylists from all over the country, it was suggested that we create an opportunity to share our gratitude with someone we knew would feel as "BIG" as we needed to be in order to give our very best to the show. I chose my father, and when I was done writing this, I called him and read it to him over the phone. It was a beautiful moment.

Dear dad. Thank you for giving me a name I can be proud of. Thank you for letting me learn through your experiences and giving me my own to grow from. Thank you for teaching me the why behind every how. For having the discipline to say "I don't know son." when you didn't know the answer. Thank you for teaching me how to grab someone's attention and to keep it. For humor and problem solving. Thank you for teaching me how to dance for all it's values - the person your dancing with, the people watching and for yourself. Not to judge a man for his dress and to respect him for it. To shake hands, look people in the eye and to be on time. Thank you for making me clever and to think complexly. Thank you for teaching me that numbers don't lie; to dig deep, to be tenacious and to cut my losses and start new with a positive attitude. Thank you for all these things and more. I understand all that you have shared, all that you have given and all that you are and I love you for all of it.

CPSIA information can be obtained
at www.ICGtesting.com
Printed in the USA
BVHW090313160722
642199BV00002B/13